My Drea

Stuart Barbour

Copyright © 2018 Stuart Barbour

All rights reserved.

ISBN: 9781983203084

www.stuartbarbour.com

Dedicated to the memory of Richard Foster

Introduction

This book is the story of my dream to fly. It is not a manual on how to learn to fly, it is about my journey of realising a dream. It shares the highs and lows, both mentally and physically of a life long vision and wish to be a pilot and soar in the air.

Contents

Chapter 1 The Dream   page 6
Chapter 2 The Dream Is Over   page 9
Chapter 3 My First Flying Lesson   page 11
Chapter 4 The Dream Is Over Part Two   page 17
Chapter 5 The Dream Is On. Again.   page 19
Chapter 6 Flight School Number One   page 22
Chapter 7 The Dream Is Over Part Three   page 26
Chapter 8 Simulator And A Real Plane   page 33
Chapter 9 Microlight   page 41
Chapter 10 First Ultra Sport Flight   page 46
Chapter 11 Headcorn   page 50
Chapter 12 Exams   page 54
Chapter 13 Crosswind   page 60
Chapter 14 Radio   page 64
Chapter 15 Spain   page 67
Chapter 16 Soria   page 72
Chapter 17 Let's Fly   page 75
Chapter 18 First Solo   page 78
Chapter 19 Fuel Up   page 83
Chapter 20 Home Time   page 89
Chapter 21 Cross Countries   page 93
Chapter 22 The Final Exam   page 100
Chapter 23 Where's My Licence   page 104
Chapter 24 I Have A Licence   page 109

Chapter 1

The Dream

There I stood at the top of the stairs, in my pyjamas. I threw my arms out on each side, standing tall and leapt out, head first. I soared down the first flight of stairs, banked left and glided down the second half, then flaring out onto the landing at three feet high I made a banking turn and headed for the living room. Whoosh! I came flying through the door and passed my father who was sitting by the fire in his chair reading a broadsheet. The paper rustled. I cried with delight, "Look Dad, I Can Fly!".
"Very good Son" my dad replied without looking up from the paper. This dream where I believed I could fly was one of many recurring dreams I had as a child. Another one involved me being in the supermarket with my mother and suddenly everybody would turn into a crocodile and I would wake up screaming. I preferred the flying dream. In fact the flying dream grew. Soon I was able to run along the ground and launch out with my arms wide open and after a short dip down, up I was scooped into the air. I loved that dream. I have always been someone who dreams and still am to this day. I look forward to going to sleep, it is almost like I have two lives, one of wild adventures and another when I go to sleep! My wife never seems to dream and I feel she is missing out. When I wake up soaked in sweat with my heart literally pounding in my chest because I have just been in a war zone in some far off land, she is quite happy that she doesn't dream. Flying was more than a dream. I longed for it. I grew up at a time when my grandparents and great aunts would tell me about their

experiences in the war: bombs going off, shutting the front door and then the door being blown from it's hinges by a huge piece of shrapnel that would have gone straight into their head a minute earlier. What excitement for an eight year old boy! I read A5 war comic stories that I collected (and my father later threw out when I hadn't tidied my room!). Both my grandfathers were in the RAF. My father's father was killed when he cycled into a tree during the blackout so I never knew him but my mother's father was a lovely Englishman with a warm heart who told me many many war stories. He once told me that the pilots would stack up a wall of chairs to separate themselves from the riff raff in the barracks. He said he didn't mind, they did an amazing job. He was too big and round to go up in planes so his job was to build targets for the bombers to practise on. He was a great man, Russell Frewin, loved by all who had the pleasure of meeting him. My father also did his National Service in the RAF and served near Rugby where we still have connections to this day. I loved planes and everything to do with them. Every birthday and Christmas I was always given an Airfix model, either a Spitfire, a Hurricane, a Wellington or a Lancaster. I would glue them together, glue my fingers together, glue them to the carpet, paint them, paint the floor and the cat, soak the transfers in a side plate of water and then stick them on the planes. I would never have imagined then that many years later I would be writing on something called Facebook - "Today while climbing from 2000-3000 ft over Brighton beach, a Spitfire flew below me". More on that later. So my love of flying was two fold. The dream that many people have, to soar in the sky and also a dream to be brave and face an enemy in mortal combat. Who would the man become? Then at the age of eight I was also introduced to the guitar. Two futures now lay before me. I loved them both.

Chapter 2

The Dream Is Over

One day I stopped being able to fly in my dreams. It was awful. I still remember being confused. I would run along as usual, jump in the air, throw out my arms and then fall flat on my face. I was confused. I would try running faster. Same result. Eventually I let it go and to this day I have never had that dream again. Perhaps this was a sign of what was to come. At the age of thirteen we moved from a lovely village in Scotland called Kilmacolm to a town where my father grew up called Port-Glasgow. We had an amazing house, Marchmont House (now a care home) that I was very privileged to spend my somewhat troubled teen years in. By now I had made the choice that music would be my hugely successful future. I no longer made Airfix planes, instead I ended up shooting them with my air rifles. Then one day I saw an advert in The Greenock Telegraph advertising the Air Training Core and my heart skipped a beat, as they say. I cut along the dotted line in the newspaper with a pair of scissors, filled in my details using a biro, put it in a white envelope, licked the tasty bit on the edge of the envelope, cut my tongue and bled on the white envelope, proceeded to lick a stamp (yuck yuck yuck) and tried to get it to stick to the front of the hand written envelope, a ceremony my children will never do, I do not miss that experience. I then ran down the steep hill from our house to the nearest postbox and waited impatiently for a response. Then a week later it came, in a brown large envelope. I was excited. I can still smell that brown envelope. I took it upstairs to my room and very carefully opened it. Wow. The front cover had the RAF insignia on it that I had stuck on many an Airfix model: red, white and blue circle. And there was a boy, a little older than me, in a uniform standing next to a real plane. This was awesome. I wanted to join and fly. Now. I read every page, every word, every detail, about trips to an airfield and more. Then on the last page it had a space for details about my local ATC saying where and when they meet. Boom! It was all over. Sunday. This was not good news for me. We went to church on Sundays, my dad was a pastor. I was gutted, the dream was over before it even got a chance. To be fair I never once told my parents I wanted to fly, if I had actually told them what I wanted to do I'm sure they would have helped me but unfortunately communication was not my best gift as a young teenager. I also had no mentors around me who had done anything like this. My careers teacher at Port Glasgow High School had one meeting with me and said I should work in the ship yards. I think he said that to everyone. Looking back on that time, my perception was that the whole world was against me, I wasn't able to express myself. My only escape was in music. I would spend every day after school playing piano and writing melodramatic songs. It was decided. I wouldn't pursue an impossible dream of being a pilot, instead I would go for the more secure career of becoming a rock star.

Chapter 3

My First Flying Lesson

A few years later I left school before sitting my higher exams. My friends and I had formed a band and managed to do some good gigs including playing on BBC Scotland's Saturday morning Untied Shoelaces show which was great - until I broke a string live on air. The church leaders were not keen on our style of music and publicly announced that what I was doing was wrong, which for a 17 year old confused teenager was pretty painful. It was also painful for my parents although I was unaware of it at the time because my world was revolving around only one person. Things changed when my father took a new job in West Sussex. I asked if I could move with them, and thankfully they said yes. My friends in our band (7th Veil) were not happy by my decision thinking I had ruined our dream, but I decided West Sussex was near London and I had a better chance of success in the music business living there. So eventually I found myself at the age of twenty spending a year traveling around on an old double decker bus doing youth work for a church in Guildford, Surrey. They had their own Youth Pastor who played a Fender Strat so I guessed I would fit in here a bit better playing my U2 style inspired songs. We had a dance group, a drama group, my new band and a magician. It was a lot of fun. We converted the bus to a coffee bar and went round schools during the day and put on concerts in the evening. In the summer we went to a Christian youth camp called Royal Week at the Royal Bath and West Showground in Somerset. A local flying club were advertising trial lessons in the shop at the show ground. I must have said that would be a dream come true because my great friend Pete McCahon announced to me he had bought me a flying lesson. Pete was a larger than life character who was the magician on the bus team. He was very entertaining and enjoyed skewering his thumb with a metal pin and shooting blood everywhere while kids screamed and vomited. Great fun. Pete would do anything for anyone and got great pleasure out of making people happy, he had a great heart which would unfortunately let him down in his early forties. After our year on a bus Pete went on to be a very successful magician including hosting a series on Channel 5 called Monkey Magic (not to be confused with the black and white Japanese series). Like all who knew him, I miss my good friend Pete, we travelled round Europe together for a while performing in coffee bars and staying in some crazy places. But it was Pete who gave me my first real taste of flying and the dream was back on. Pete managed to blag a car from someone on our campsite (we couldn't take an old London double decker bus) and off we headed to the "Airport". It was in fact a very uneven field with the grass cut short for a runway. And there it stood in all it's glory, an old Cessna 150 from the 1970's. I was met by someone who can only be described as an old RAF veteran. He was wearing a flight suit and had a white curly Biggles moustache on top of a huge grin of yellow teeth. I on the other hand was an over confident twenty year old in jeans with white baseball boots and the piece de resistance - a very cool leather bomber jacket!

"Are you ready to fly?" He beamed at me.
"I was born ready!" I replied. He laughed. We climbed on board and got strapped in. After checking the headsets he

started her up. Awesome. What a sound. I was high already. He then proceeded to teach me how to taxi the plane using the pedals and not the yoke, this was the first thing I learned about flying. Press with your toes on the top of the right pedal and the right wheel brakes causing the plane to turn right, press the top of the left pedal and you turn left. We taxied to the runway.

"Are you confident enough to take off?" he asked.

"WHAT? Are you completely mad? Take off? You have to be joking!" I said. In my head.

"Absolutely" I replied.

He instructed me to push a lever all the way in that looked like a large choke lever from a car (remember those days?). He then instructed me to gently pull back on the yoke and to hold it there. I listened to every single word he said. Intently. I followed his every instruction exactly. This discipline would do me well years later in my flying lessons. I don't remember anything about the pedals at this point so I guess he was pushing the right pedal to stop us drifting left because of the propellor wash running over the plane and affecting the rudder. All I could see out the corner of my eye was this old RAF fellow leaning back into the corner of his seat with his arms folded. Mad I thought, barking mad. Then another thought hit me. We're flying along at dear knows what speed with our nose in the air and there is a fence at the end of the runway. Just as I was picturing our wheels whacking into the fence and smacking our nose back on the ground, we took off. We were airborne. I was flying a plane! A small bead of sweat ran down my forehead and into my eye.

"Watch out for fighter jets".

"What?" I whimpered.

"Fighter jets. They do low flying practice in this area, if we get caught in their wake we will spin out of control and crash".

"??????"

My eyes were popping out of my head looking for fighter jets! Old RAF bloke just grinned. We levelled off somewhere above 1000ft and the lesson carried on. He taught me how to get the plane in trim using a small wheel which I would turn in the direction I was pulling or pushing the yoke. This helped make flying easier on the arms. We worked hard at flying straight and level. We did some simple turns trying not to lose height. Then we flew over the campsite where my friends would all be waiting full of excitement to wave to me and take pictures of one of the biggest moments of my life. Except they weren't. There was the bus, but no one else. Later they would apologise and explain they waved to an earlier plane and took pictures of it. Looking back I think they were probably not as excited as I was and were off elsewhere doing their own thing. RAF bloke then decided I was too confident for my own good and proceeded to show me a stall. During the stall and while racing towards the ground, he gave me lots of information about what was happening and how he would soon recover it. I didn't hear a word. Terrified. I had no concept of how long it would take to reach the ground at this angle and speed and I didn't want to find out. After what felt like far too long he recovered the plane. I let out an involuntary laugh.

"Ok" he said "You have done really well for a first lesson, do you want to land it?" I opened the door and jumped out.

In my head.

"Of course" I replied as if he had asked a stupid question. He let out a laugh. Possibly involuntary. We were flying along the coastline which I would learn later was the base leg of the airfield circuit. The runway (grass field) was on our left.

"Turn left when you think it's right to line up with the runway. The longer you leave it, the steeper the turn". Wrong thing to say. I am now a fighter pilot, piloting a spitfire about to make my strafing run. I had practised this diving turn many a time when I was a boy flying down the stairs, turning into the hallway and whooshing through the living room past my dad reading the paper. I was ready.

" Ok that's far enough, turn now" he said. He was still smiling.

"Reduce your speed" At some point he brought down stage one flaps.

Pick a point on the runway and keep the plane headed for it. I have never concentrated as much in my entire life. This was nuts. He was nuts. I was nuts! There's that fence again. As soon as we were over it he shut the power and we glided down.

"Pull back on the yoke". Now he unfolded his arms and helped.

"More. Hold. More. Hold. Back. Hold. Hold". Dunk. The rear wheels were down.

"Pull back. Hold" Then the front came down gently. We were nowhere near the grass runway strip by now but thankfully it was a big field. I apologised for not being on the runway, after all that flying I felt like I had failed and let him down for believing in me. He just laughed. We taxied back, got out and I shook his hand. For too long. Awkward. I will always be grateful to Peter McCahon for his generosity and reigniting my dream.

Chapter 4

The Dream Is Over Part Two

To this day I remember every detail of that first lesson. I have retold the story countless times, about the door not shutting properly, seeing light through the edge of it it even when it was supposed to be closed, the smell of the old plane, the old RAF bloke, how the plane must have been like a toy to him because he was happy to let me fly it. I later learned it was a pretty standard first lesson apart from the landing which is unusual on a first lesson. And so, two years later at the ripe age of twenty two I realised my career choice was not working out. I was not a multimillionaire with numerous hit records so I would just have to go back to my first choice of becoming a fighter pilot. I vividly remember when I had my one and only conversation with my dad about joining the forces he told that I wouldn't be able to take the discipline. Those words had stayed with me and made me question myself but I put the doubts aside and headed to the recruitment office in Guildford, I think it was on Castle Street. I was wearing my bomber jacket. Sorted. I was met by a stiff upper lip to which I announced I wanted to sign up right away and become a fighter pilot.
"How old are you?" he fired.
I bowed to his disciplining tone snapped to attention and hailed "TWENTY TWO SAH"
Ok, I may not have said "sir" at the end, but I felt it.
"Too old".
Crash and burn. Shot down in flames. I hung my head and limped out of the door. The walk of shame. Stop! No way! I am not defeated. I turned and stormed back in and said

"There must be something you can do?"
"There is" he replied. Victory?
"I could send you down to take a test to inquire about becoming a navigator".
"Where does he sit?"
"Behind the pilot".
It was all over once again.

Chapter 5

The Dream Is On. Again.

I took myself off to music college and studied full time at The Guitar Institute in London, qualifying Best of Year 1996 which was a proud moment in front of my wife, my sister, her husband and my mum and dad. I was even awarded a brand new guitar on graduation day. Look Mum and Dad, the boy done good. But it wasn't flying. I went on to work hard as a working musician playing lots of live gigs and studio sessions. I even got the chance to play guitar at the old Wembley Stadium before it was knocked down, I played at Hamburg football stadium, I performed solo at the Royal Albert Hall, Nottingham Concert Hall and many more. I also spent a good number of years playing guitar and producing albums for Alvin Stardust who became a close friend. But it wasn't flying. When I played guitar for Alvin we sometimes gigged with The Rubets and their lead singer had a licence and his own plane. Jealous. Then I had breakfast at a gig somewhere with the lead singer of The Troggs who told me he was terrified of flying and drove everywhere to all the gigs. He then started telling me about crop circles. I took a phone call. At the age of forty five I found myself in a caravan park at Le Pas Opton in France, I was singing and playing guitar at a Christian holiday camp and my wife and kids were getting a free holiday in a beautiful part of France. Then, whilst relaxing at the poolside, I downloaded an app called X Plane. I had been avoiding flying, strangely, it was just a bit painful even now, anyone I mentioned flying to had a story about someone they knew who was a pilot for EasyJet or BA, even our new neighbours in Ifold told us they owned their own biplane and had named their daughter after Amelia Earhart, the famous pilot who was the first lady to fly solo across the Atlantic Ocean. I watched on the BBC bit by bit how Prince Harry and Prince William became helicopter pilots. Then I heard how King Willem Alexander of Holland had been secretly flying as a commercial airline pilot for twenty five years. It's a hobby apparently. I tried to be happy for the privileged life they were having. My wife's cousin, whom I had known since he was a kid had borrowed £50,000 from his parents and went to the USA to get his commercial pilot's license. His parents both worked for British Airways, so there is your mentoring. He is now a very successful BA pilot. It seemed like everyone was flying and living the dream except me. I was jealous. £50,000? I could never afford that. It wasn't going to happen. Yet here I was again looking at aviation. I got hooked on the X Plane app, trying to land a Cessna, impossible on the app yet I had done it in real life a very long time ago. I made an announcement. I told my wife that I was going to get my pilot's license before I was fifty. "My pilot's license." As if there was some license out there with my name on it and I just had to earn it. If only it was that simple. Then I woke up one morning and I was fifty. I was depressed. Very depressed.

"What do you want to do for your birthday?" my wife asked.

"Nothing" I replied and went to work. My colleague's had bought me a cake and had chipped in £50 for me, £1 for every year. Great. I tried to be grateful and thank them. I was very very unhappy. Failed. Again. A few days later I had a "chance" conversation. One of my colleagues, Ben, was talking about his dream to fly. Another friend shared how he nearly joined up to become a fighter pilot but changed his mind and became a very successful cameraman which he is glad about now because the Gulf war broke out one year after he nearly signed up. By this time I had stopped telling anyone any of my dreams. I had even stopped telling anyone my amazing "first flying lesson" story.

"My friend has his PPL and has offered to take us up if we all chip in" says Ben. Pah! I was about to leave the room with a small cloud of rain above my head like you see in cartoons when he went on to say, "I've looked into it, it costs £7,000 to get your license". I stopped dead in my self misery. £7,0000? Not £50,000 I still can't afford it I thought to myself as I jumped on my one year old Harley Davidson Street Bob and headed for home. I thought about it the whole way home on my one year old Harley Davidson Street Bob. "How can I raise £7,000?" I asked myself as I parked my one year old Harley Davidson Street Bob in the garage. I entered the house and sat down and began to think hard. Eureka! The Harley was on ebay that very night. The dream is back on!

Chapter 6

Flight School Number One

Inspired by my friend Ben, I opened a bank account and called it "Flying Fund". In went the £7,000 from the sale of the Harley and then I sat down with my wife and told her what I wanted to do.
"Go for it" she said, "at least it's safer than riding motorbikes!"
Motorbikes are another obsession of mine, this Harley was my thirty eighth motorcycle since the age of thirteen, there is another book to be written of adventures (and crashes) on bikes. My good friend, the wildlife artist Richard Symonds, once suggested to me that we sell our sports bikes (he was on a Kawasaki 600 and I was on a Honda CBR600 at the time) and buy microlights. He thought that we would be safer flying them than our current riding on the bikes. It was a fair point, we were having more than our fair share of "incidents" however I didn't fancy hanging from a kite in the sky. Richard went on to buy a para glider and regularly flies it round Surrey. When Clandon House in Surrey went up in flames he flew round it and filmed it, the footage was shown on BBC news. Finally years later I was following Richard's advice, selling my bike to fund my flying dream!

My house was between two small but popular airfields, although we were not close to the airfields we were under the direct flight path between them. Every day I could watch small planes flying back and forwards and wish I was up there. Still, better to be down here wishing you were up there than up there wishing you were down here, or as my good friend Andrew Dancy puts it - a successful pilot is one who has the same number of take offs as landings. Now, with the money in the bank, I searched the Internet and found the website of my nearest flying club, only twenty minutes drive away, and sure enough, there was list of costs which came to around £7,000 to get "my" private pilot's licence. I was excited. There were pictures of people standing next to a Cessna and a caption saying they had just done their first solo flight. I was impressed. I jumped in my car and drove straight there. After parking I entered the building and climbed the stairs, followed the signs and entered the flight school. I recognised the chap on reception from the website. I was eager. He was on the phone. I stood there for a few minutes in anticipation and then started feeling a bit awkward. He was still on the phone. I sat down. He hung up and proceeded to write some stuff down. Finally he looked up, pen still in hand, and said "Can I help you?"

I could see he was still eager to write whatever important stuff he was writing and I was obviously a bother but I didn't let that deter me, I knew once I announced I wanted to be a pilot that he would drop his pen and give me his full attention.

"I want to be a pilot".

The pen remained in his hand.

"It's very expensive" he said " have you paid for your parking, you'll get a ticket if you haven't".

I should have worn my bomber jacket to show him I was serious. The same bomber jacket I wore on my first lesson thirty years ago. The same jacket I wore when I tried to join the RAF.

"£7,000" I said, "I read your website".

"Oh, it will cost a lot more than that, at least £10,000" he retorted.

"You bloody liar!" I shouted. In my head. I don't like swearing.

"Ok" I said, trying not to be put off. I told myself he was being hard to get because he didn't want me to waste my time, I'm an optimist. It's quite annoying really, it means I never imagine anything going wrong which unfortunately means a lot of disappointments. With hindsight I should have got up and walked out there and then but I didn't, I sat there looking at him and I kept on smiling. Finally, I had his attention. The pen went down.

"Ok, why don't you book a trial flight and see how you get on?"

"I'll book three" I said.

He paused, "Ok, book three then. When do you want to fly?"

A year later at a different flying school I would be asked the very same question with a very different outcome.

"Now" I said. It was a beautiful day, there were Cessna planes sitting outside the office, lets get on with it for goodness sake.

"Ooh" he offered, rubbing his chin looking up at the beautiful blue sky.

"I know it looks nice," it does I thought, "but it's hazy up there, there is no clear horizon".

Pah, I thought, but he was probably right. So I booked in my three lessons for the following week. There was an Italian flying instructor standing by the window, he told me

I would be flying with him. He looked friendly enough. I was given a list of Pooley's books that I would need to buy and study, I ordered them online as soon as I got home. This was it, finally the dream was on!

Chapter 7

The Dream Is Over Part Three

The Pooley's manuals arrived and I started studying the first one, Flying Training. I bought a notebook which I have to this day full of all my study notes. I drew a Cessna on the first page and labelled all the parts, it was the best way of learning for me. I learned about ailerons, pitch, drag, thrust, yaw, angles of attack, PAT (power, attitude, trim), I devoured and loved every bit of it. There are four basic forces affecting a plane in flight - Lift, Weight, Thrust and Drag. Lift is what the wings need to do to get you airborne which is obviously working against weight. Drag is the resistance force on a plane when it's flying which thrust needs to overcome if you want to fly, add more power and you get more thrust which also gives you more drag. Flying a plane is all about getting these forces in balance for whatever manoeuvring you are doing. After all these years it was finally happening. I read through the first lesson so I would know what to expect on my first logged lesson. This would include getting familiar with the aircraft and learning the basic principles of flight. Learning about the three axis; the longitudinal axis which is a line from the tail to the nose of the plane, the lateral axis which runs from the tip of one wing across to the tip of the other wing and the vertical axis which runs from the top to the bottom of the plane. The plane moves through these axis. Pitch in flight uses the lateral axis, roll is on the longitudinal axis and yaw (veering from left to right or vice versa) is movement about the vertical axis. Using a combination of the yoke, rudder pedals and thrust of the engine you control the plane in flight. The first lesson would be learning to use these controls to fly the plane straight and level on a given direction, for instance flying on a heading of 240 degrees at 2,200ft at 90 knots (which turned out to be a lot harder than it sounds, if you change speed you change height etc). Then we would do basic climbing and descending followed by medium and level turns. Reading the Pooley's manual made sense, I had covered a lot of this on my first flight all those years ago, it suddenly dawned on me that the old RAF chap wasn't being blasé, he was just going through a first lesson which obviously hasn't changed to this day, well, apart from the landing bit maybe. I arrived early but didn't enter the office until five minutes before I was expected. I am always early. I was introduced to my instructor. It wasn't the chap I was told I would be flying with, instead it was a larger, perhaps more serious man. We went into a smaller room. He handed me my first log book and told me to put my name in it.

"Can I borrow a pen?" I asked.

He paused, looked at me, then got up and went out to get a pen. He wasn't impressed. And this is how would continue. Where is my bomber jacket when I need it? He used a red wooden model plane to describe what we would do on our first lesson. When he spoke about something I recognised I would offer my input, "Right rudder to stop the plane going left on take off," he would pause while I interjected my knowledge from what I had studied and then carry on once I stopped talking. As we left the office he put on a yellow hi viz jacket.

"Should I put one on?" I enquired, everyone I had seen on the sacred apron (where the planes are parked) wore one.

"No" he said dismissively.

On my subsequent lessons he would tell me to wear a hi vis. Out we went to the plane. I turned and looked at the people in the café. It felt good. I had sat there in awe and watched as people went out to the planes to fly. Now it was my turn. I savoured the moment and donned my sunglasses, the theme from Top Gun blaring in my imagination. We walked round the plane checking for anything out of place, checking for tyre creep and cleaned the screen. We didn't check the fuel which I was disappointed about, every walk round I had seen on youTube involved them checking the fuel. Detail. I need the detail. He said it had been checked on the previous lesson so I didn't need to check it again. The plane was old. The panels were slightly bent around the rivets and the main cog that turns the propellor was red with rust, a lot of rust. When I finally sat in the chair the door wouldn't shut properly and when it eventually did I could still see daylight through the edge. All similar to that flight when I was twenty so I didn't panic. Well not too much. The cockpit felt much smaller than I remembered but then I realised my new instructor may have been a bit larger. He handed me some headphones with two jack plugs on them and told me to plug them in.

"Which plug goes in which hole?" I asked assuming that would be important.

"Just plug them in down there" he replied.

I was nervous now, he wasn't happy. I wasn't happy. I plugged them in and just hoped they were in the right way round. Later I would buy my own headphones and discover the jacks are slightly different sizes so you can't get them

mixed up. This would have been helpful information at the time and was all that I really needed to know. We followed a printed checklist procedure and started the plane. He told me to check the brakes as we taxied the plane towards the runway but when I pressed on the top of the pedals he instantly barked "Not that hard, I don't want you damaging the propellor on the ground". How on earth I was supposed to know what level of braking was necessary for testing I have no idea. He then changed the channel on the radio and listened to a recorded message and wrote down some secrets on his sheet of paper. I would find out about listening to ATIS on the radio in my own time, not his. He instructed me to keep the wheel on the yellow line while we taxied to the hold. This should be one of the easiest parts of flying but it never went well on any of the three lessons that I would have with this instructor. I was constantly expecting it to go wrong and for him to point it out to me and consequently it would. After getting clearance, we lined up on the runway, pushed in the throttle and off we went.
"Don't take your hand off the throttle, we don't want to lose power and crash" he barked.
"Don't grip the yoke so hard".
"Don't release the flaps so fast, that's agricultural".
"Don't treat my plane like that".
"I said 2,500ft not 2,550".
I wasn't enjoying this, I was tense, couldn't do anything right, this is not the way I learn. I remember watching a programme on TV once about Gurkhas in the British Army, they were trained totally different to other soldiers, their officers didn't shout and scream at them and tell them they were useless, instead they just told them what to do

and they did it. They followed the instruction. That just makes sense to me, why would you argue with orders from your commanding officer? If you don't like it then train to be an officer and give out your own orders. Being barked at and being told "No, not like that", made me tense and unable to fly properly. After landing and wobbling back along the yellow line to park up I asked him if he would take a photo of me in the cockpit. He didn't reply, he just carried on tidying up his seat and sorting out his stuff. When he was ready, he huffed and took my iPhone and duly took the photo. I wondered if I was the only person to spend a considerable amount of money on a flying lesson and want to have a momento of the occasion. Back in the office we duly filled out my first hour in my new log book. This should have been a memorable moment but I had very mixed feelings about it. I left the office, walking past the main instructor who was talking on the phone and too busy to say goodbye. I got in my car, happy not to have got a parking ticket, and headed for home.
"How was it?" my wife asked when I got home.
"Good, yeh, good" I replied unconvincingly.
It wasn't good.
I studied hard for my next lesson, I wanted to get my money's worth. After our pre-flight talk he sent me out (with a hi vis jacket on) to do the walk round. I hadn't done this on my own before so was a bit unsure of what to do. I read the procedure that I found on a sheet of paper inside the door which said to turn on the master switch and the pitot heater and beacon light. I did this, then walked round the plane, checking the pitot was hot (to avoid icing up when flying), the beacon was on, checked the flaps, tyres

etc.

"No, no, no!" came the voice of doom, "you'll flatten the battery," and so my second lesson continued. After the lesson I tried to build bridges.

"What are you doing this evening?" I offered.

"Going on a simulator".

"Oh, have you been on the large simulators at Burgess Hill?" I asked trying to make some sort of connection.

"I've been on simulators all over the world". he replied.

I gave up.

Lesson three started disastrously but made up for it all by a very special moment. Once in the plane, grumpy chops handed me the keys and told me to go through the startup procedure. When I tried to put the keys in I couldn't get them to go in the ignition switch, I tried and just couldn't get them to fit.

"Not already" I thought, "am I really that useless?"

Without a word he brushed me aside leaning his large body over me, and grabbed the keys. He fumbled. And fumbled. I started grinning. He looked at the label on the keys.

"I brought the wrong bloody keys" he snorted, "I don't know why I do this".

By this point I was fed up with him.

"Perhaps it's to help people like me who want to learn to fly" I said. Out loud, not in my head this time. He snatched the keys and off he went to exchange them for the correct ones. Ho hum. Funny as it was, this wasn't the special moment I was referring to. Eventually we wobbled down the yellow line, did our pre-flight checks, got clearance and headed off to the wild blue yonder for an hour of deep joy. Then halfway through my lesson it happened. He told me to look out of my window below us. And there it was flying underneath us. It was beautiful. I was finally smiling and very thankful to be there at that moment and that time. That evening I updated my Facebook page with the following statement: "Today while climbing to 3000ft over Brighton beach a Spitfire flew underneath me along the coastline".

My friends left some lovely comments recognising what a special moment that was for me, but in reality, the dream was over. Again. I hadn't enjoyed my lessons. I left my jumper in the plane on the last lesson but I couldn't care less, I was happy never to go back there. When I left the office the chap who I originally booked the lessons with never said a thing to me. Never called me to book more lessons, to see how it went, nothing. I had my log book now, with three hours logged. Another dream not going to be fulfilled. I was depressed. I immediately went on ebay and bought a Harley Davidson from West Coast Harleys in Scotland. Flying bank account now empty. When my good friend Matt, who is plane crazy, saw me on the bike, he pointed at it and said "That's your PPL right there". Ouch.

Chapter 8

Simulator and a Real Plane

A few weeks later I had a "chance" conversation. Raefn is a sixteen year old lad who tells me he flies for up to three hours some evenings.
"What?"
"Simulator".
He went on to tell me that he flies 747's with different people on the internet. They all run their sims and log in online and fly all over the place and communicate with Air Traffic Control. It turns out that people studying to be air traffic controllers are online with them and are directing all the traffic, it's not a game, they are all learning and take it very seriously. My interest was peaked. For some reason I had always thought of simulators as games but slowly it was dawning on me, this is actually how commercial pilots learn to fly. In fact every programme I have watched about aviation has involved simulators. Doh! I went on ebay that evening and very soon I had acquired a Cessna yoke and pedals, switch panel, saitek radio and two more computer screens. I bought X Plane 11 beta version for my Mac for only $59 dollars, an absolute bargain. I then proceeded to go through all the training sessions that a pilot had kindly put online. Why I hadn't got into this sooner I do not know, but thank you Raefn Webber. I should have done this before going for my flying lessons, it would have made it a lot easier, I would understand how to use the instruments properly, how to fly a circuit, take off and landing speeds, use of flaps etc etc.

About this time, a friend who had seen my pics on Facebook of me next to the Cessna contacted me. She told me her brother teaches near where I live. It was another one of those success stories. His dad had bought him a lesson when he was sixteen, he got totally hooked and is now a captain for BA, flies all over the world and when he's not doing that he has his own plane that he flies and when he's not doing that, he teaches. My friend is a really kind person so I assumed her brother must be too. I contacted him on Facebook and sure enough, he was very happy to answer all my daft questions. Even though I had spent my funds, I still couldn't walk away from the dream, so I arranged to meet him for a chat. I took my twelve year old son with me this time and drove down to his club. The welcome I got this time was a million miles from my last experience. It was a very relaxed atmosphere, I was welcomed at the door with a smile. Unfortunately the pilot I was meant to meet (my friend's brother) had to leave due to a family emergency and wasn't there, so instead someone else showed me and my son all round their club house. He then took us into the hangar and showed us some planes including the Piper Warrior PA28 that I would learn on if I chose to fly with them. He even turned on the glass screens. I was shocked, is that ok for the batteries (after my previous experience)?.

"Yeh, it's fine" I was assured.

I liked these people, they were happy and relaxed and clearly loved flying. I asked about prices. It was expensive. I tried to haggle ie: if you book five lessons at once is there a discount.

"No, we're the cheapest around" I was informed.

I booked a lesson. It was back on. I headed home and downloaded a PA28 for X Plane and started flying. My music studio was now turned into a flight simulator. I knew I would be flying from Shoreham Airport this time so I made a flight plan in X Plane 11 from Shoreham EGKA to the nearest runway I could find which was EGKL. This proved to be quite fortuitous some months later. EGKL turned out to be a small grass strip in amongst trees and small buildings. I made this flight over and over, trying to follow all the radio instructions on the way which seemed like a whole new language to me. I psyched myself up on the day of the lesson, got my best cap and sunglasses ready, had a quick flight on X Plane and then the phone rang. The lesson was cancelled due to the instructor having a family issue. I was gutted. This would prove to be the way of many lessons in the future but would end up being the reason for me going on the adventure of my life, more on that later, first the PA28.

On the day the lesson was re-scheduled I headed down to the club with my best cap and sunglasses on yet again, at least I could try and look like a pilot. At the clubhouse it was all very relaxed, my instructor asked to look through my log book to see what I had done. I asked if I could bring my GoPro, which again was not a problem. All good. We headed out to the plane and she told me to go ahead and do the walk round. I had a good look over everything, checked for tyre creep, blocked pitot, any dents or missing parts. I told her it all looked good but I hadn't checked the fuel. She asked me why not? I informed her my previous instructor said I didn't need to after it had been done earlier in the day. She wasn't impressed. She took out the small fuel drainer and explained to me how to use it. I had watched people do this on walk rounds on youTube but hadn't been trusted enough with this procedure on my earlier lessons. Now I was in the club. The fuel was ok. I was then shown how to check the fuel level too by taking the cap off and looking in the tank in the wing to see what height the fuel was at. She then showed me how to remove the engine cover and asked me to check the oil, if it was low I was to go and get oil from the hangar and fill it up. Now I was being trusted with maintenance too! Sounds funny, but when someone treats you like you are competent you start acting like it too. This was already starting to feel a lot more comprehensive than my previous experience. With the walk round complete we climbed aboard and went through the startup procedure. After she made a radio call to the tower I was instructed to taxi the plane to the hold.

"Here we go again" I thought. I was determined to stay on the yellow line, I had practised on X Plane, it wasn't difficult. I was nervous. She didn't say a word, just looked out her window and seemed totally relaxed. I taxied the plane to the hold with the nose wheel dead on the yellow line (ish). No pressure. Good result. At the hold she took over, it was a strong crosswind and she turned the plane into it and put the brakes on. I was a bit disappointed as I was sure I could handle the plane already. Ever the optimist. My instructor fiddled with the radio and wrote down some secret "ancient chants" that mysteriously came through our headsets. I would later learn this was AFIS or ATIS, which is information about the wind direction, runway in use etc, info that a pilot needs for taking off or approaching the airfield. After our pre flight checks and radio call we entered runway 06. I was instructed to follow her through on the controls as she took off. Another disappointment, I had taken off four times now and many more times on the sim. She knew there was a crosswind. We did some basic exercises revisiting what I had been taught before, climbing descending, turns, straight and level flying and also avoiding clouds which was fun. She told me she was happy with how I flew and said I was very confident in my use of the controls. Me? I was totally blown away. This was a real plane, wings underneath, glass cockpit (ie a computer screen with the instrument panels on it), it was also faster and more stable, much easier to turn, I loved every moment of it. Eventually she told me to take us back along the coast towards the airport. This was my first lesson in how much wind affects flying. I pointed the plane along the coast line, I was flying! Before long the coastline was getting further away from us which was slightly confusing, the plane wasn't going where I was pointing it. After a while of my drifting the plane, she took control and led us back to the airport. With the wind so strong I was actually very happy I wasn't going to be landing this time. We crabbed in with power on, power off, power on and so on, I was amazed she got us back to the tarmac, we were now being blown all over the place the nearer we got to the ground. Back in the clubhouse I was pumped, this was it, it was definitely on again. I booked in lots of lessons and headed home very happy. The new Harley was on ebay that night.

After the dust had settled and the adrenaline gone I had a look through the cost of getting "my" license at the new school. I got out my calculator. Forty five hours of flying the PA28 worked out at £8,640. Forty five hours is the minimum requirement, the fact is it could take up to sixty hours apparently. Landing fees worked out at £1,458, touch and goes another £378, test fee £185, exams £500. My Harley was worth £7,000. The dream was ending yet again, I could sense it slipping through my fingers. My flying experience really was up and down. I sat down with my wife and went through all the figures, she encouraged me not to give up yet but to continue with the lessons and see how it goes. I can't see "how it goes" it's all or nothing. That evening she came into the studio to find me packing up all my X Plane controllers, radio, yoke, pedals, screens and everything being listed on ebay.

"I see you've made up your mind already" she said. I said nothing and headed back into my small world of depression. I could hide it, I had failed before, I knew how to smile and deflect the questions that would come. That's my problem, when I am excited about something and I want everyone to be excited about it, I share it with everyone, including Facebook, but now I am realising that I need to just be quiet in the future because this hurts. Bad. I even had my kids flying the sim.

"Where is the flight stuff gone dad?"

Pain.

The flying school called me the next day to cancel my next flight for some reason or another, I told them to cancel them all and apologise. They are very gracious which is not surprising, they have been genuinely helpful and kind from my first Facebook chat with one of their instructors to my first meeting with them and eventually my first flight, I would gladly recommend them.

I still had £7,000 in my flight fund from selling the Harley (again) but this time instead of replacing it I decided to spend the money on taking my family to Disney, a bittersweet holiday to the place where "dreams come true" but would always remind me of the dream that never came true. So my wife and I headed off to a holiday booking agent in a nearby town to us. I told the guy in the shop that I wanted to take my family to Disney.

"How much do you want to spend?" He asked.

Why is everything so complicated?

"How much does it cost?" I asked.

"Hmph" and raising of eyebrows followed.

This wasn't going to be easy.

We were informed it depended on when, where, how long blah blah blah blah. I gave him the dates. He then proceeded to look at flights online, and parks for tickets, then apartments. This was ridiculous I thought to myself, I could easily be doing this myself at home, anyone could, what I wanted was a simple - "yes sir, here are a choice of combination packages that we have ready for you and will take out all the hassle, plus we get a great discount so can do it cheaper for you as well, and here are the prices". I was surprised there was nothing like that on offer and we ended up leaving with a brochure. It may not have been that bad, I might have just been feeling grumpy. On the journey home I was sensing my wife wasn't as enthusiastic about this plan as I was trying to be. I assumed she would be very keen and happy that I was finally doing the "right thing" and putting my family first, also, she had worked at Disney for a year when she was at University and she had a great time there so I assumed she would be over the moon to be heading back again.

"What's wrong?" I asked.

She pointed out to me that the kids were already having four holidays this year (two were due to my work as a musician where they all came along), and also that I absolutely hated queuing which is what we would spend our time doing at Disney and finally that I needed to learn to fly or I would a pain in the neck to live with. She didn't quite say it like that, we are always polite to one another but I'm pretty sure that's probably what she was inferring. This shook me up a bit, I was a bit caught up in my own emotions and not totally aware of the effect I was having on everyone around me. I also loved her for it, she stopped me from heading down a road that wasn't the one I had meant to go on. And I love her for it because she meant it. So once again, I had to re-think, how was this dream ever going to become a reality?

Chapter 9

Microlight

It was now springtime and I sat in my garden watching light aircraft flying over my house with a bittersweet smile. I was genuinely happy for the people flying in them but longed to be up there myself doing the same thing. I opened this month's copy of Pilot Magazine. During one of my times of "it's on!" I had wandered in to WHSmiths and bought a copy of Pilot. I absolutely devoured it and hoped one day I would understand what they were talking about in all of the articles. They had a special offer on for a one year subscription for eighteen pounds. This was a great offer but also very risky. I knew if I took up the offer and then at some point was not able to become a pilot then this would be a monthly reminder of failure. In a moment of optimism I went online and took up the offer. Now I was paying the price. I wasn't flying and here was a magazine telling me about everybody who was flying. But there was something unusual about the front cover this month, it had a picture of a stunning looking and very sporty red two seater plane with the words something along the line of - "We review this new microlight from the east". A microlight? I was confused (not unusual). To me a microlight was a small seat under a kite with one bolt holding them together, not really my idea of fun personally but obviously very popular nonetheless. I read the review, and the specs of this "microlight" were way better than the Cessna I had flown, faster and a lot more fun. I had to find out more. It turns out a microlight is just a class of aeroplane, it's the weight that matters, it needs to be no heavier than 450kg unless fitted with a parachute for the plane, then it can be 472.5kg (since writing this it may be changing to a whopping 600Kg). This weight is very crucial and there is one make of microlight that is unpainted because the paint would take it over 450kg. Having a plane classed as a single engine light aircraft under 450kg is a lot cheaper to maintain and a lot cheaper to get a licence for. With a bit more research I realised that in America they call them Sport Planes and I had been watching them (with envy) on a great programme called The Aviators. Whenever they visited various aerodromes there were always lots of these small two seater planes coming in that they referred to as Sport Planes…. "even the sport planes land here". I always thought they looked like a lot of fun. My interest was peaked, there was hope on the horizon………...it may be on again. In the same issue of Pilot I read through all the adverts at the back of the magazine and one of them grabbed my attention. It was for an airfield in Kent offering to help you get your EASA PPL for only £3665 in a Cessna 150. This was less than half price compared to the prices at my local airfield. It was a two week course and just seemed too good to be true. It would take me two hours to drive there through one of the busiest parts of the M25 but I made a plan, I would get two weeks off work and drive up with my caravan and camp on the airfield or nearby. Again, my wife was onboard and told me to get on with it, so I contacted them and asked if it was a good plan and was it actually realistic to get "my" PPL in two weeks. The email reply wasn't good. This was a new thing they were trying and it all depended on weather and also most people need a lot more hours than the minimum required. In other words - no. Angst. Ok, I'm not giving up. I read a book about someone who went to Florida and did it in a month so there were still options out there, I just needed to find them. There was another advert. Do all your exams in one week for £500. I emailed them - is this realistic, can I really get through all my exams in one week? In my head I was keen for this to be true but in my heart this seemed impossible, I was already studying the Pooley's manuals and it was hard going and time consuming. "Yes", they replied and I could stay at the airport for £35 a night in a local motel, no one had ever failed. Apparently. That bit made me more than a bit suspicious, I had read online of many people having to re take at least one or two exams. It was a long way to go and a big commitment, I needed time to think. I then had another discovery that would change everything and make it possible for my dream to fly become a reality at last! I sat down with my kids for supper (small snack before bed, not a meal called dinner. Just thought I'd clear that up, it may be a Scottish thing, can be embarrassing if you get confused and invite someone round for supper and they turn up with a bottle of wine and are dressed up a bit for dinner and are not impressed with toasted bread!!). We channel flicked for something short to watch that would be fun for everyone, they were bored of watching You've Been Framed repeats which always had me laughing and them reaching for their phones or similar gadgets. I clicked on the Red Bull Channel app on my Apple TV, we had watched skateboarders on this channel before when my son was getting into skateboarding and I thought there may be some similar crazy programme of people going on amazing adventures. There it was. A small picture of someone on a flexwing microlight flying into the sunset, it was a great pic. I had to click. What unfolded was the most amazing adventure of two friends (well, they were at the start of the programme anyway) attempting to fly microlights across Australia. The thing was they had never flown before, they just decided they were going to learn and then go for it. One of them, who was totally unreliable and made for good television, had to sit his last exam on the day they were leaving! It was a great series of shows put together of their adventure that always had us on the edge of our seats and always finished with a cliffhanger so we had to watch the next episode. This wasn't some big budget Red Bull series, it was clearly them just knocking it together with the help of some talented friends. I loved it. I was hooked. I was going to fly. My daughter was not so impressed though, the series made her never want to see her dad fly one of these crazy naked kites in the sky. Ever! It took some time to explain to her that I was going to fly a "light sport plane" it's just that we call them microlights in the UK which puts them in the same class as the scary kite planes. And so the search began on the internet. As it happened, finding a microlight school near me wasn't as easy as I had hoped. There were none at my local airfield and I would later discover that this may be because EASA PPL flying schools are not happy with the cheaper competition. After much searching, I found someone teaching on a very cool looking two seater plane, the lessons would lead to getting an NPPL (National Private Pilot's Licence with a Microlight class). The price was good, £120 for a 1 hour lesson with minimum of 25 hours required. This was good. Very good. I contacted them. They replied by email that this was the old price and they now had a new website I needed to look at. I looked at the new website which advertised a trial 30 minute lesson for £49. Awesome. I clicked on the link to book it and it took me to a Paypal payment page and asked me to pay £69. Oh for goodness sake. I emailed back and forth and got mixed messages, including that a one hour lesson included schooling on the ground so not all flight time etc blah blah……….goodbye.

I found a link from another webpage which kept teasing me about another school near me, but when I tried the link it never worked. Very frustrating. Then I had a flash of inspiration, search for the school on Facebook. There it was. Flight Sport Aviation, in all its glory with a beautiful picture of an Ikarus C42 Sport Plane and a link to their website. It turns out this was a fairly new school to the area and the website was new too which is why it wasn't coming up in my Google searches. I emailed them, ever hopeful. This time I got a normal response. The prices were similar to the earlier Microlight school I contacted and I could do a trial lesson for £90. I wasn't interested in any trial lesson, I knew I was going to do this, let's fly! I booked my first full lesson so I could start getting my hours in immediately. It was on. Again!

Chapter 10

First Ultra Sport Flight

So the day came, I was excited, I drove to the small grass field about thirty minutes from my house. It reminded me of the grass strip field I had had my very first lesson on thirty years beforehand. It was good. But there was something else that was familiar and I couldn't quite put my finger on it, I wouldn't realise what it was until I got back on X Plane. My first flight in the C42 was on April 15 2017 with a chap called Chris. Chris was the examiner for the school so a good person to go flying with. He had a quick look at my logbook and then said "Let's go". We had a quick walk round and time to get familiar with this new plane. I climbed in and it was very different from both the Cessna and the Piper Warrior but it felt good. It had one stick in the middle and basic instruments, the throttle is a small stick that sits in front of and between your legs, there is also one in the other seat. We taxied to the end of the runway, did our pre-flight checks and then lined up to take off. Chris told me to follow him on the controls. At first I was disappointed at not getting to take off but when we started hurtling down the grass strip bumping about all over the place I was very glad he had control, a grass strip feels very different from a smooth tarmac runway. And then we were off. This was it, I was flying again, if you haven't flown in a small plane it is hard to explain the experience, it just brings an instant smile to your face, you are free, you are flying. It wasn't long before Chris said the words I wanted to hear, "You have control".
"I have control". I replied.

And so we went through all the manoeuvres I had learned before. Flying straight and level, climbing, descending, turns, climbing turns.
"You fly well" Chris said.
My world stopped at that moment, time stood still, the one thing I somehow longed for without realising it was encouragement, someone who knew what they were talking about to say, "hey, you can do this". Suddenly my flying was even more confident, I wasn't gripping the stick as tight as physically possible, I started to relax and focus. Chris went on to teach me about using the compass and using the term UNOS - understeer North, oversteer South. The reason being that the compass doesn't respond as well as you need during turns and you need to stop before the heading comes up when turning North and go past the required heading when turning South, when you settle, the compass catches up and is hopefully somewhere you need it to be. Chris said another way to turn is to use landmarks, for instance, if he tells me to turn the plane through one hundred and eighty degrees then I look out of the window and see a landmark in the distance in line with the wing and then turn the plane round and line up the other wing with the landmark. He pointed to a large block of flats that was under my left wing (a long way in the distance) and said turn the plane round one hundred and eighty degrees and put the other wing there. I confidently turned the plane after first lifting the wing to check it was all clear, added power to keep it at the same height and stopped with the other wing lined up with the block of flats. Chris looked out. "Nowhere near it" he announced. I laughed, I probably was just in front of it by an inch. This was good, he wasn't

annoyed or being miserable, he was just saying it as it is which was very helpful, I now knew what he expected of me. We headed back to the airfield and he talked me through the landing, we came in with stage one flaps at sixty knots. Again, like my first landing thirty years ago, there was a wire fence at the edge of the runway, the runway was also short compared to my last four lessons, it even dipped in the middle and the picture in front of me seemed all too familiar. But there was one thing different. The plane was pointing into the wind. We had a cross wind which naturally turned the plane into it at our slow sixty knot approach speed. Chris said nothing. I adjusted power for our height and approach to the field and kept the plane pointing right. I waited for him to tell me when to straighten up but he kept silent. Eventually I made the decision to line up as we came in to land, I lifted the nose to flare and then Chris finally spoke.

"OK, don't land it, keep it off the ground".

"What?!" I thought. "Does he want me to go round? Do I add power?"

And then I realised what he was doing. He was making me hold it off the ground longer so we would have a gentle touch down. And that is what happened. I was hooked. As I approached the end of the runway I had a welcome committee, my wife was dropping some of my kid's friends back to their house nearby in Lewes and they had all come in to watch me land. This was a great feeling, having my kids seeing me do something I had talked about for so long made me feel very emotional. I was smiling. Richard, who owns the school and would soon become my flying instructor and good friend, was standing next to my wife and commented to her "He looks very happy." And so the adventure began, I booked in thirty hours of lessons and the next two months turned into an amazing adventure I couldn't have even dreamt of.

Chapter 11

Headcorn

I bought a very old Honda Nighthawk motorbike to get me back and forth to the airfield avoiding the chaotic traffic jams as the A27 goes in to one lane just after Lewes towards Eastbourne. The brakes on the bike were interesting and would keep me alert. I hadn't ridden a bike with brakes like this since probably my first road bike at sixteen, a Honda MB5 that I acquired from someone called Shuggy One Eye (he had two eyes). If I remember correctly, I swapped an old drum kit, an electric guitar and an air rifle for it. He got the better and safer deal. Anyway, over the next couple of weeks I was back at the airfield on my dodgy bike as often as I could, covering all the exercises in the training manual but a strange thing kept happening, as I was riding to the airfield I would start to question my ability to go through with this, I would start asking myself if I was clever enough to pass the exams, could I remember everything, was I actually intelligent enough, did I have the skills to actually fly a plane? It was really odd and I continually had to try and shut the thoughts down. I started making statements out loud in my bike helmet (and steaming up the visor when it was raining which didn't really help)
"You can do this!"
"You are a pilot"
"You are intelligent"
"You are in control of the plane"
Etc etc and on and on, but this really took me by surprise, I had always been so confident in the past, maybe it's an age

thing, I still don't know, but it happened continually throughout my whole training time. After a few lessons with another instructor I had a lesson with Richard who owns the school. Richard is an evangelist for flying, he absolutely loves it and it is very contagious. We went through a few exercises and he then announced to me, "Ok, you can fly, let's go and do some circuits." Wow! Circuits!!!! I had sat in the cafe at my local airfield and watched enviously as people went round and round doing circuits. Circuits teach you how to take off and land again. It is also how you land at an airfield you visit, you join the circuit. Basically, you take off upwind, then at about five hundred feet turn left into the crosswind leg (if it is a left circuit, obviously it would be right if it is a right circuit but left is preferable because the pilot sits in the left seat and has the best view from there) and climb to usually one thousand feet at which point you turn left again and fly the downwind leg parallel to the runway maintaining one thousand feet. When the start of runway is approximately forty five degrees behind you, you turn left again into the base leg and start to reduce your height back down to five hundred feet at which point you turn left into the final approach leg where you are perfectly lined up for landing. Hopefully. So we headed off to Headcorn, about thirty minutes away. This was my first airfield to airfield flight, up until this point I had always landed at the same airfield I had taken off from. This also meant radio communication. Terror! Richard told me what to say and I did my best.
"Headcorn radio, this is Golf Charlie Foxtrot Alpha Victor".
"Golf Alpha Victor pass you message".

My mind went blank, what message? I'll have two black coffees and two bacon sandwiches please? Richard saw the colour disappear from my face and he made the reply. "Don't worry" he said, "You'll get it eventually".
Failed. We got to Headcorn and Rich talked me into the circuit and I lined up to the massive grass strip, if you can't get the plane on that then you are in trouble. I landed smoothly and smiled. I then taxied the plane (no yellow line to follow on a grass strip) to the Flightsport Aviation's new office at Headcorn and was met by Tina who turned out to be comedian Joe Pasquale's daughter. She was happy to see us and told us all the goings on at the airfield. At this point there was a loud whoosh above us, "What on earth is that?" I thought. It turned out it was nothing on earth, it was parachutists above our heads. "You've got to be joking" I said. Sure enough, there is a parachute school there which is very popular. Where do they land? At the end of the runway. Of course they do, why wouldn't they? Tina then proceeded to tell me about some awful parachuting accidents that had happened there in the past and about someone who died, told me I should google it. Great. I'm not going to do that.
"You ready?" Asked Rich
"I was born ready!" I replied.
And off we went. I don't know how many circuits we did but it was superb, I was grinning from headphone to headphone. Take off, climb, turn, turn, turn, turn, land and so on and on and then .... panic.
"Rouge chute" came the call on the radio.
I had just taken off, right next to where some of the parachutists had already landed.

"Where?" I shouted.

"Directly above us" Richard replied.

"What?!!!!!!!" "What do I do?"

"Fly the plane" he replied calmly, "He will get out of the way".

Welcome to Headcorn circuits.

Chapter 12

Exams

My ten year old daughter is a gymnast and is very dedicated to it to the point of obsession. Yes, you can guess where she gets it from. She told my wife and I she wanted to move gyms to one at K2 in Crawley, about thirty minutes away from us. The sessions are two hours on a Monday after school, three hours on a Wednesday after school and two hours on a Friday after school. A nightmare? Au contraire, it was perfect! I have to study for exams, this would be a great time to study with no distractions so I signed her up. (And again, here I sit, writing this very book at K2 in Crawley while my daughter tumbles through the air at Hawth gym club). So every lesson I came armed with my A4 notebook that I bought from WHSmiths a year ago and also with my copies of Pooley's flying books. I laid them out on a table and read and read, made a lot of notes, studied non stop. I was always joined by some of the other children's mums who would sit beside me watching their kids at gym and funnily enough never once asked me what I was doing but helpfully told me every time Holly was about to do some special tumble or vault or whatever so I could look up, watch and smile at her as she landed and looked round for affirmation from her dad. It worked well, everyone was happy. Eventually I emailed the flight school and said I was ready to start taking the exams and they said I could do them when the weather was bad and we couldn't fly which made sense. Then one day the following week it was raining so Rich text me and asked if I was free to do an exam now? This was a big step for me, I had visualised

taking the exams, I had read other people's Facebook posts of them taking flight exams, I had imagined posting to one of the groups - hey, passed my first exam! and getting lots of likes and smiley faces just like the other people had. I was nervous. "I'm on my way" - I text back. I jumped on my rattly old Honda and blasted off to Richard's house. I left in such a rush I forgot it was cold in the evenings, it was still April after all. I followed Rich's directions to his house and it turned out to be right next to the Harley shop I used to use. I tried not to look through the window of the shop, probably because I didn't want them to see me, full faced helmet, a top box! oh the shame. I pulled up to electronic gates and then rode down the driveway of a very large estate. Flying was good business I thought to myself. I was now frozen and started shaking. This was not good, to be fair I was nervous but not shaky nervous for goodness sake, I was going to look like a weirdo unless I could control this. Once I got in the house I knew I would be fine and could warm up. Rich's partner Shellie gave me a warm welcome and invited me in. Unfortunately it wasn't warm enough, I was still shaking.
"Would you like a drink?"
"Yes please, a very hot coffee" anything I could warm my hands on.
I sat two exams that evening and all the studying paid off, thankfully I had learned the correct stuff. Phew. I was elated. I was on my way, this was the taste of success I longed for and I liked it. I was still shaking though, which funnily enough I was glad about. I had told myself I was shaking because I was cold but there was a horrible thought somewhere deep down that it was nerves which would be

truly awful, the fact I was still shaking after passing the exams brought me relief that it was just the cold. Now we relaxed and I mentioned to Rich that he lived in an awesome place. He agreed with me but said it was a hassle to look after all the grounds and the other properties. There was a large swimming pool/gym that they hired out to someone who did swimming lessons for parents and kids, a cottage they would rent out to hen party weekends and then the ghost house………….. The ghost house. This is not the usual discussion you have with someone when making light conversation after a stressful experience ie taking exams.

"What ghost house?"

Apparently there is a house on the property where someone had died seventeen years ago and the house had stayed exactly the same since they died. No one had ever been to it. No one. "No one?" I thought. That's just too much.

"I have to see it" I announced.

"Really?" Rich replied with a wry smile.

We headed off down through his, I would call it garden but I think "grounds" is more appropriate. We went through bushes and trees and down a small path. The sun was setting. What on earth was I doing? I started to question whether this was some sort of weird ritual that new students go through and I was about to walk into something crazy. I didn't know Rich but I know he is a character and full of life or as Shellie puts it "He has the luck of the Irish". And suddenly there it is. A house with all the vegetation starting to consume it. All completely untouched, no one had been in there for years. It was too much temptation.

"Can I look closer?"

I saw a new expression on Rich's face, it was a look of apprehension, up till now he had been a fearless leader, master of the skies but at that moment he was not sure.

"Really? Em, ok" he replies.

I made my way through the foliage and came to the window. It had moss on it which I rubbed out of the way. Peering in the window I saw a sofa, newspaper and cup on a table, all covered in dust, a bookcase was full of books and, oh, what were they? Yes, I remembered them, video cassettes. Richard told me he didn't want to stay long because this place gave him the creeps. He meant it, he didn't like this place at all, it freaked him out , I was seeing another side of his character. I looked through another window and the kitchen was just as it would have been. Dishes on the strainer, now filthy with dust, old food boxes on the side board, untouched for seventeen years. There were long briars growing through small gaps in the door frame somewhere and then yuck! What is that on the ceiling? It took me a few seconds to focus and then I realised what it was. It was a thick layer of cobwebs which must come down about one foot, I had never seen anything like that before, I was totally engrossed when all of a sudden…..ROARRRRRRRR! I froze and Richard screamed! I turned round to see what looked like a crazy bald man with a white beard staring at us.

"You complete %$£&***!!" Richard shouted.

The crazy man burst out laughing. I had no idea what was happening. How did I get here? Deep breath and relax. Scott is a good friend of Richards, he popped in to the house and Shellie told him where we were so he decided to scare the living daylights out of us, and he did. We walked back to the main house laughing, Rich and I laughing in that "I am still in shock" sort of way. It was now late. I was still cold and started to realise I hadn't eaten in hours or told my wife and kids that I had passed my first exams. Richard and Scott were heading off on another adventure to advertise the flight school by putting up a huge banner on a local roundabout late in the evening when no one was watching. At that point I could have gone with them and bonded like crazy men do when doing crazy things but I was totally spent and for the first time made a sensible decision to wish them well and head for home to some warmth and celebration with my family.

Thankfully the rest of the exams were not so full of exploits. Studying at K2 while Holly was at gym worked well. I headed in to each exam feeling unworthy, not intelligent enough, questioning my memory and came out of each exam happily surprised. All except one. Navigation. I had read in online flying groups about Navigation being the tricky one so I studied extra hard. I spent a whole Saturday just doing triangle of velocities. This one would take a bit more effort. I sat the exam at the flight school main office, Richard gave me a sheet to prepare a flight plan, a question sheet, then looked at his watch and told me to start. I read the first question and panicked. I could feel my head starting to whirr. I didn't know the answer I told myself. I tried to slow down.
"It says you're supposed to supply me with a map" I said to Richard.
He looked at me with a look of "What?" He then turned and pointed to the huge map on the wall, the one that has

always been there, the same one we have used before our flights to see where we were heading and to check air space and what height was safe and legal to fly at. Arg!!!!!!! I followed the instructions on the map, "What is the name of the village twenty three miles along your route?" I measured twenty three nautical miles with my ruler. THERE IS NO VILLAGE!!!!! I'm losing it. I could feel it creeping up on me. Failure. I could sense it's smile and laughter of derision. You complete and utter failure. Go home. Watch your kids faces. Should have gone to Disney. I prayed. "God help me". Then I sat down and took a deep breath. It was at this point I looked at my ruler and realised I was using the wrong scale. 1:500,000 instead of 1:250,000 What a muppet. Back to the map and there was the village. I did my calculations and filled in the form. My answers started to correlate to what is on the exam paper. I took it slowly, one question at a time. I know this! I can do this ! Failure - I kick your butt!!! And I did. I passed.

Chapter 13

Crosswind

One morning I arrived at the airfield and Richard asked me how much time I had, I told him I was free all day. So instead of jumping in a plane we jumped in his BMW to go and deliver some vouchers to the local hang gliding club. When we got in his car he started pressing buttons on a computer screen in the car. I asked him what he was doing and he said he was checking the oil pressure. I laughed and asked if we needed to do a walk round the car first as well. He didn't laugh he just kept checking the car systems. "Ok" I thought. "How much did this car cost?" I asked. His reply was a number I wasn't expecting. We then pulled out onto the road towards the hang gliding school and whack!! I was thrown back in my seat as the car accelerated at warp speed, I expected him to raise the flaps as we took off but as soon as the journey started it stopped, uber breaking and eyeballs popping out of head moment, we were at the hang gliding school. I popped my eyeballs back in. Richard is full on, it's all or nothing, no in between. We entered the club and were given a very warm welcome, clearly Richard is well known and liked here, a lot of banter ensues. And coffee. They were packing up chutes and harnesses for some mega trip somewhere but decide now was a good time for lunch and asked Rich and myself to join them. He looked at me and I said - "Let's do it". After a very short trip at light speed we were soon all sitting down enjoying a farmhouse meal. One of the guys owns the hang gliding club, another was an ambulance helicopter pilot and another a hang gliding student. I quickly began to realise there is a strong sense of

community amongst aviators. They all do something most people only get a glimpse of, either from sitting in the back or watching from below. The conversation consisted of incredible stories of crazy adventures in between a lot of laughing at each other. It was a good lunch. We then said our goodbyes and headed back to the airfield, it was time to fly. In a plane, not Rich's car. We got in the plane and headed off to Headcorn to do some more circuits. Yeehaaarrr! I was pumped. Thankfully I landed smoothly at Headcorn because there was a great reception of hundreds of people there. It was an open day and the Spitfire was out doing fly by's and letting people sit in her and have their picture taken. It felt funny taxying along the side of the runway with lots of people watching from the other side of the fence, kids waving, I waved back, Rich laughed and just shook his head. I couldn't resist the feeling of "yes!" I'm on the inside, I'm not on the outside watching it all happen, but strangely enough at the same time I wanted to open the window and shout "Don't just watch, come and fly, it's awesome!". I didn't. I taxied past the Spitfire and smiled to myself thinking what a brilliant day this is. Then I looked at a huge poster with a picture of a spitfire on it and a sign saying - Spitfire experience from £390. £390!!!!!!!! Oh my. Really?????? After parking the plane we went for a coffee with the other instructors, Tom and Chris. I mentioned the sign and £390. They laughed. "It will cost ten times that".
"But the sign says £390" I protested.
"Go and sign us up then".
I got out my phone and checked out the weblink on the poster. £2,700 for a twenty minute flight. Gutted. They were right. I watched the spitfire take off for a short flight

with someone £2,700 worse off sitting in the adapted rear seat enjoying history. Rich came over and joined us and told me that he had just been in to the control office and that there were crosswind gusts of up to twenty knots and none of the flying schools were flying. The C42 is only rated up to fifteen knot crosswinds.

"What do you want to do?" He said.

"Are you asking me or telling me?" I replied.

He smiled. "I'm asking you".

"I want to fly" I replied. By now I think he knew what I would say. Rich then pointed out to me that because no one else was flying all the students and teachers would be sitting having coffee and watching anything going on, so it would be good advertising for his school. Unless I cocked it up! I smiled and said "Let's do it." What followed was the most awesome flying lesson ever. The wind was strong and we were light but I was going to land that plane safely no matter what mother nature threw at me. I did some landings with the plane turned into the wind, crabbing it in and straightening up on touch down. I did some landings with the wing tipped into the wind and subsequently one wheel touching down before the other. A couple of times Rich went to grab the joystick to take over as we were thrown about by a huge gust but then left me to it because I had reacted at the exact same moment to counteract the wind and stabilise the plane. I had gained a lot of trust in Rich by now, I had been in the plane with him when he cut the power at three thousand feet above the airfield and then proceeded to lose height and bring us safely onto the runway. He knows how to fly this thing better than most so I knew that if I messed up we would be safe. Great way to learn. I don't know how many circuits we did but I was still high with adrenaline when we finally landed and stopped. A pilot who was visiting from Spain said to me "Some nice landings there, well done." Which means some not so nice too, I know, but I took the compliment anyway, it was a good day. We headed back to Deanland and filled out my logbook. I was now up to twelve hours and fifty minutes in the Ikarus C42, I had four more hours, one on the Piper and three on a Cessna but all that mattered now were my hours in the C42.

Another time I was booked in for lessons with Rich and he asked me if I wanted to join him at Headcorn to make a promo video for the flying school. So off we went to Headcorn where we were met by friends of Rich including a camera man, a drone pilot and comedian Jo Pasquali. I spent the day there helping out wherever needed, cleaning the panes etc and having a good laugh at the capers as they put together a short film. When the film was eventually posted to social media I read the credits and discovered I was now promoted to "tea boy". Oh the glamour of aviation.

Chapter 14

Radio

I was still struggling with making radio calls. I would say - "Deanland traffic, this is Golf Sierra Whisky taxing to the hold runway twenty four" at which point my instructor would say to me "Two four not twenty four". Embarrassingly this was blasting out of the loud speakers at the airfield where there just happened to be a group of pilots sitting around chatting. And Laughing. I would make the initial call to Headcorn en route and then my head would go blank when they replied "Pass your message". The thing was I was focusing so hard on flying the plane, keeping the right height and speed etc straight and level, my mind struggled to take in more information. I needed a plan, so a plan was made. I realised that I had six journeys every week in the car with my daughter Holly going to and from gym club so I decided that Holly was going to become the air traffic controller. Thankfully I had turned up at the airfield one day for a lesson when the weather decided it was not going to happen so instead I asked Tom, my instructor for the morning, to write out some radio communications to help me practice. I then printed this off and stuck it on the dashboard in my car, I would read out my message and Holly would reply. It went like this.

I would start the car and announce
"Deanland traffic, this is Golf Charlie Delta Sierra taxiing to the hold, runway two four".
Then as I pulled off my drive way I would say

"Deanland traffic this is Golf Sierra Whiskey entering runway two four for immediate departure".
And as we drove off
"Deanland traffic, this is Golf Sierra Whiskey exiting the circuit heading west at two thousand three hundred feet".
After a couple of miles
"Shoreham tower this is student Golf Charlie Delta Sierra Whiskey"
Holly - "Student Golf Sierra Whiskey pass your message"
"Golf Sierra Whiskey is an Ikarus C42 from Deanland to Goodwood, one person on board currently over Lewes at two thousand three hundred feet, estimate your overhead at two zero, Golf Sierra Whiskey"
Holly - "Roger Golf Sierra Whiskey, QNH 1023, Maintain two thousand three hundred feet, no conflicting traffic, call overhead".
"QNH 1023, maintain two thousand three hundred feet, will call overhead".
After a few miles
"Shoreham Tower, Golf Sierra Whiskey overhead".
Holly - "Golf Sierra Whiskey"
After a few more miles
"Shoreham tower, Golf Sierra Whiskey switching to Goodwood, thanks for your help".
Holly - "Golf Sierra Whiskey, have a good day".
A few more miles
"Goodwood Information this is student Golf Charlie Delta Sierra Whiskey"
Holly - "Sierra Whiskey pass your message"
"Sierra Whiskey is an Ikarus C42 inbound from Deanland with one person on board currently over Arundel at two

thousand three hundred feet request airfield information".
Holly - "Roger Sierra Whiskey, runway in use is one zero, right hand circuit, surface wind is 240 at 12 knots, QNH1023 QFE 1021 call overhead"
"Runwayone zero, right hand, QFE 1021, Sierra Whiskey, will call overhead".
"Goodwood information, Sierra Whiskey overhead"
Holly 'Roger Sierra Whisky, call downwind".
"Goodwood information, Sierra Whiskey downwind runway one zero"
Holly - "Sierra Whiskey"
"Goodwood information, Sierra Whiskey final approach runway one zero"
Holly - "Sierra Whiskey"

We did this over and over and over, Holly took her role very seriously and enjoyed having a role in my training to be a pilot. Bit by bit it would slowly sink in and we wouldn't have to read the script, I began to work out the information I had to give and also what I needed to repeat. It would have to sink in quickly for the adventure that was ahead.

Chapter 15

Spain

Over the following week I psyched myself up getting up at 6.45am so I could get to the field in time for my lesson only to get a text cancelling it because of the weather. It was very frustrating, I was all too aware of how quickly you can forget what you've learned if you don't keep up with the lessons. This meant part of my time would be spent recapping on what I should already know. I told Richard how annoying it was (British weather) and he said quite nonchalantly "Lets go to Spain for a week then and do an intense course".
I laughed. Again, he wasn't laughing.
"Do you want to fly or not?"
"Fly to Spain? Actually fly to Spain? In the plane?"
"Yes, I do it all the time" said Rich.
"That'll cost a fortune"
"It will cost the hours you fly and thirty euros a night for hotel with breakfast included" he said. This just seemed impossible to me. I talked to Andy (my wife, remember? Andrea). As usual, she didn't hesitate, "Go for it".
We looked at the diary, it wasn't possible, I had gigs, work, Holly to gym, school pick ups etc etc. Then my son Kyle stepped in, "I'll pick up Holly from school for you". Then Andy stepped in, "I'll work from home and take Holly to gym." They were on my side, what a family!!
Richard was keen to go Saturday but I had gigs on Saturday's so I told him I could do early Sunday morning and get back on Friday, would that be enough to do everything I needed? Rich reckoned we could do it and

cover everything left to do for my course. It was on.

I got home late on the Saturday night (early hours of Sunday morning to be exact) and couldn't sleep. At a last minute check I realised I couldn't find my euros. I emptied everything out all over the floor and started to get stressed, I didn't need this, not now. I turned the house upside down looking everywhere. Nothing. I then sat down in front of my computer and thought what do I do now? As I sat there I noticed a strange edge to my keyboard, I lifted it up and there was the cash. It was now very very late, not a good start. Five am came too soon, only three hours of rough sleep. We got up and got dressed and rushed out the house and heard a ping ping ping. My wedding ring was on top of my bag, Andy rushed out of the house with it and it fell off the bag and bounced away. We never found it (and still haven't). This was not a good sign. When going through the flight plan for the trip with Rich had told me that we would be flying at around ten thousand feet over the Pyrenees and I would need to "man up." I had flown through turbulence in West Sussex and been a bit surprised a few times but he said that was nothing compared to what we would be flying through. This spooked me a bit and made me hug my wife and kids for a few moments longer when saying goodbye. The thought even popped in to my head to write goodbye letters……….just in case. I didn't. Now I'd lost my wedding ring just before going, not good. Rich phoned me while we were on the way.
"Where are you?"
Don't tell me he's stressed out too. We got there at five forty am, our flight plan was to take off at six am but the fog was starting to rise now as the sun came up and would

probably cover the field very shortly. We put on our life jackets and I said goodbye to my wife and thanked her. She filmed us flying away. This was it, we were really doing this. I flew the plane along the coast towards Dover before turning right and heading over the channel at the shortest point between England and France. I looked out to my left and right and saw the sea and a few container ships. I couldn't stop smiling, all the stress of getting here, losing my money, losing my wedding ring, it was all gone, this was stunning, I was flying a plane across the channel. Rich was smiling too, this was his environment. He started singing to me. I asked him to stop. As we approached the coastline I told Rich I had something for him that Holly had prepared. I then handed him a sheet of paper and on it was listed all of the airfields on our route over France that we could land in if we got into any trouble. It is a great document that I will keep. When planning our route I had laid the map down on our living room floor and drawn a line from Le Touquet to Angers to Biarritz. Holly then followed the line and carefully made note of every runway on our route.

The views from the plane on this part of the journey were amazing, flying along the coast and then over land and on to Angers. We originally planned to land at Le Man but the MotoGP was on that weekend and the air space was closed. Flying over the MotoGP and watching Valentino Rossi racing really would have been the icing on the cake but it was not be. Richard made me make radio calls to LARS (Lower Airspace Radar Services) but no one was awake it would seem. I was both happy and disappointed when I got no reply. Happy that I didn't have to make sure I got all my calls correct but at the same time sad that I didn't get the experience of using the radio. After a couple of hours I needed a wee. The next hour and half was very long. Eventually I got my chance to talk to Angers Airport and follow their instructions (and reply correctly) and finally get on finals to the very long runway. This was my first landing at a main airport. The runway was huge. As I came in to land Rich pointed out the runway was so big it followed the curve of the earth and I had better not land on the threshold but make sure I landed on the proper part of the runway. I added power. As soon as pulled off the runway and stopped, the gendarmes approached us.

"Can I see your licence" I was told. Not asked.

"I am a student".

"This is a long lesson" he replied.

He has a point. Just then an Air France passenger plane landed. It was enormous, I thought it might blow our plane away, next to that thing I can see why the gendarmes were slightly bemused with us. We refuelled, went to the loo, drank coffee and I took off again on this massive runway, it took me forever to fly to the end of it before heading off South. What followed was a beautiful flight along the coast of France and a similar landing experience at Berritz, I'm not sure the airports were that keen on us being there but I loved it. Standing at Berritz I could see them. They were huge. It was hot and sunny where we stood but they had snow on them. They were dark and terrible and beautiful all at once. It was the Pyrenees. It was time. We had run our tanks dry on the last three and a half hour leg of the journey so we could change fuel from mogas to avgas which apparently doesn't expand at heights over six thousand feet. Eventually I entered the runway and got us flying again, heading for the mountains. We climbed to around eight thousand feet and chose a pathway through the mountains. It was absolutely stunning, I completely forgot all about manning up, this was one of the calmest flights I had ever had. Thank you God! Seeing the mountains this close, dazzling greens blue lakes and snow peaks was genuinely awe inspiring, I was still pinching myself to believe this day was actually happening. I had the plane nicely in trim and we had no turbulence so I took my phone out and started to film some of the scenery. Rich asked me if I wanted him to take control of the plane but I told him not to touch it, I was paying for this and was going to fly it the whole way. He laughed. This flight was shorter and after an hour and a half we were looking for our runway. Eventually it appeared in the distance, I tried making radio calls but got no answer so we flew over it, checked the windsock to see which runway would be in use, I made our calls to let any traffic know where we were and then brought the plane down gently on to runway two seven at Soria Aerodrome in Spain.

Chapter 16

Soria

Richard was warmly welcomed by old friends. Romain is a bit of a celebrity apparently amongst the aerobatic community and was clearly looking forward to spending a week hanging out with his crazy English friend. Romain and his fellow pilot, Phillipe, are both from France but have come to Soria for the week to teach aerobatic flying and there was no shortage of people wanting to learn. They had hired an aerobatic plane and it was booked out solid the whole time they were there. There was also a glider pilot who was going to spend the week giving gliding lessons and he was also fully booked up. For the moment everyone was all hugs and handshakes but some of the friendships would be put to the test as the week progressed. Then there was Santi who was the boss of the aerodrome, he welcomed us and offered us some food which Richard and I kindly accepted, a bacon roll and a coke each. By now we realised how hungry we were and this snack went down well, at least it did until we met a rotund grumpy chap who proceeded to charge me twenty euros for the food. A bit odd I thought but I was happy to be there in one piece so I paid up for the food that Santi had offered us. Later in the week equivalent snacks would cost five euros. We sat outside the cafe on the apron of the aerodrome. I could feel my body still swaying after nearly nine hours flying in a small plane. There were a few people sitting around and the occasional person walking their dog came past too. It was a beautiful evening and I sat back to take in the view and the experience. Vultures were circling above us and I pointed them out to my new friends. The atmosphere changed, like a dark cloud had landed, they gathered round and looked down on their new foundling in pity and the the scary stories round the campfire began.

"Vultures have a three meter wingspan, if you fly underneath them they will attack. Just this week a flexwing was dive bombed out of the sky in Southern Spain. Not long ago a family of four was killed when they flew their Cessna underneath a circling vulture. The bird swooped down at them and smashed in to the cross support beam for the wing causing it to break off and the plane to come crashing to the ground".

This was all going so well. Now I was terrified. The more I looked, the more vultures I saw. Worse still, when I got flying the next day I discovered that the local council had built large nesting areas for the birds to use in the field right next to the aerodrome. Madness? It got worse. Later on during the week we found Mr Grumpy (the one who ripped me off on our arrival) throwing out all the old bread from the day out the back of the cafe to feed the vultures!! He will surely be losing his job soon. A young lady wearing dungarees said hello to me and asked what we were doing here. I proudly told her that I had just flown from England to the Spanish aerodrome. She seemed suitably impressed with my achievement. I told her I was here to do an intense training course to get my licence.

"How many hours have you flown?" She asked.

"I must be up to about twenty now" (after our epic journey).

"Well done" she said.

I asked her where she was from and what she was doing (I

thought she may be working in the cafe or something). She said "I am from Poland and I am here to learn aerobatic flying with Romain".
"Oh. What do you do for a living?"
"I am a commercial pilot".
I excused myself and left.

Santi ran an airfield in Requena which is where Richard teaches flying through the winter months. Apparently he was taking over this airfield now as well and trying to turn it into a working successful aerodrome. It was built over ten years ago when the whole area was undergoing a massive investment from the government but then in 2008 when the markets crashed the money dried up and all the work was stopped. It was very strange after landing in small busy grass strips in the UK to be here with this massive runway which was not being used. The local area has large unfinished buildings which were going to be art or music venues, They looked like three large sails which were excellent landmarks for finding the runway when I would be flying the local area later in the week. There were empty car parks and roads blocked off or fenced off, it was all a bit strange really.

By now it was getting late and I was tired, we managed to blag a lift to the hotel where we were staying which was about five minutes from the airfield. I was pleasantly surprised. The room was large and very comfortable, I couldn't help wondering if someone had heavily invested here when all the development was taking place and was now happy to have any guests at all.

Chapter 17

Lets Fly

We were all up early the next morning. Once breakfast was consumed all three schools were happy and ready to go. Richard teaching a newbie, Romain and Philippe teaching commercial pilots how to have extreme fun in a plane when not carrying passengers and the gliding school who were going to soar. Like the vultures. Arg. The vultures. We got to the airfield at 9am. Mr Grumpy roared passed us in his car on the apron shouting at who knows what as he headed down to the hanger where we all had our planes stored overnight. We were last to arrive yesterday and consequently our C42 was the last one in the hangar and the first one that needed to come out. Mr Grumpy walked up to it and proceeded to take hold of the propellor and start to pull it. Richard did his nut.
"STOP! Get your hands off my plane".
He was mad. Mr Grumpy just waved it off and moved on to the next one.
"Who the hell does he think he is" Richard seethed. Actually we had no idea but have to assume he had been hired by someone at the aerodrome. We proceeded to carefully and correctly manoeuvre the aircraft out of the hangar and onto the apron where I did the morning checks. We needed fuel. Guess who does the refuelling? Yes, Mr Grumpy. I started singing "Happy day, oh happy day".

Eventually we got fuelled up and headed off for our first morning of lessons in beautiful weather. As soon as we were flying that smile returned, I was happy and felt totally blessed to be where I was in that moment. I was even more happy when I realised the vultures were not out in the morning because the thermals hadn't started yet. The morning went well, Richard was constantly giving me non stop instructions, I tried to relax and soak it all in. All too soon it was time to land and have some lunch. We were served by Mr Grumpy's wife (he has a wife?), she was very helpful and even appeared to be happy. I was surprised when it didn't cost twenty euros today. Odd that. It was starting to heat up now and I started to see them. Not one, not two, but loads of them, starting to circle round and round, higher and higher, I looked up and there were more of them. Everywhere. That feeling came back, I recognised it now quite well. Fear. Why was I doing this? I am used to scare stories. Having ridden motorbikes nearly all my life I always meet people who say something like -"Oh you ride motorbikes? My neighbour's son's best friend once knew someone who heard about someone's sister who was killed on a bike once." It's like a disease, spreading these stories. I still ride bikes, but aviation is a bit different, there aren't any escape routes. I tried to put it out of my mind as we headed out for our afternoon session but my eyes were hard wired for the vultures. We started doing circuits. Above us I realised it's not the vultures I needed to watch for, it was the aerobatics going on. Their plane was tumbling, spinning, looping and doing everything I didn't want to do with my plane. It was amazing to watch, especially since they are above "the box" and we were flying round it. As it started to warm up, the thermals made this session hard going, I focused very hard getting the plane to turn while were getting thrown about a bit. Rich told me that if a bird came at us from the front I should pull up so it hits the under belly of the plane and not the propellor. This was a timely instruction because on our very next circuit that is exactly what happened. One minute it was all clear and the next there was a bunch of swallows right in front of me. I pulled up hard expecting to feel a bang of some sort. Nothing. We looked at each other and laughed. Slightly nervously, at least they were not vultures. Later when we were back on the ground Richard told me that Effing Mike from Manchester was flying out to join us and have lessons with Richard, and would I mind EasyJeting home instead of flying back. He assured me I would get everything done that I needed to which included me getting ten hours solo flying in while we were there. I said it was fine as long as I could achieve what we had set out to do that week and then asked why he was called Effing Mike.

"You'll soon find out" Rich replied.

Chapter 18

First Solo

Later that evening a local news crew arrived at the airfield and started filming all the goings on. It turned out it was good news for the local area and people were asking what was going on. Richard bought me a Soria shirt with the runway numbers on each arm, 09 and 27. Now at least I looked like a pilot and hopefully would fit in a bit. I wondered if I was finally going to get to do my first solo flight soon. Your first solo flight is a big deal, I regularly watched student pilots on Facebook putting up film of them doing their first solo flight and there are smiles and very often tears too. I had imagined flying solo ever since my Cessna lessons. I can do it on X Plane for goodness sake, how hard can it be? We did more circuits in the evening and Rich said "Right, I am not going to say anything, you just fly the circuits".
This was it. I was sure. But..........on every circuit Rich stepped in and gave me instructions. Nuts! I know it's not yet. Then he did something completely mad. He said to me "Don't mind me, just carry on flying". I knew that was not a good thing. He was up to something. He leaned across me and started to unscrew the instrument panel. He then proceeded to take my map and put it over the instrument panel, tucking the top in to it to keep it in place.
"Fly the plane" he said.
Now, you have to understand that in all my training and in everything I have read up until now that your instruments are everything, especially letting you know when you might stall, you need to know your speeds and your height,

temperatures, pressures, fuel, arg!

"Your instruments should confirm what you already know, you shouldn't have to rely on them all of the time, you need to learn to feel what you are doing" explained Rich. I realised I was smiling as I continued flying so thankfully I must have been enjoying this, I was concentrating too much anyway to allow fear to pop in. And so another day finished. Still no solo flight. That evening we all met up in a restaurant, we were a good little community now. I was sitting next to an aerodrome owner, a commercial pilot and someone from Holland who teaches flying. Everyone had a story and everyone was very happy to be there. Our meal cost us ten euros each. Mr Grumpy is a thief with his twenty euros for a bacon butty. I forgive him. The next morning when I went for breakfast, the locals all said "Hola" and showed us the local newspaper. Our gathering was all there in words and pictures, we were local celebrities now. What a laugh. At the aerodrome I met Mike. Mike was a character, I quickly discovered how he got his name. His language was very colourful but also very funny. Over the next three days we spent a lot of time together as we both learned to fly but as our conversations played round in my head I started to panic that Effing Mike was influencing me. I told him I was worried that when I got home and met my wife at the airport and she asked how it was, I might reply "Effing great!" She would not be impressed. He laughed.

After lunch (five euros, not twenty! but I have forgiven him) Rich and I headed off for another lesson. Just after taking off Rich pulled the power and announced "Engine failure!" For a moment I nearly shouted "No it's not, you just pulled the throttle back!" Thankfully I didn't as I quickly realised this was a test, not only that, I realised this was a test before going solo. It was going to happen. First thing you do when the engine fails? Fly the plane. I put the nose forward so we didn't stall and then gently turned to the right and told Rich I was going to land in a grass field I was heading for. As I descended, Rich pushed the throttle forward and said "Full power, climb away". He did this a few more times and talked through the procedures for engine failure and forced landings. Then we went back to circuits and once again he said "Right, you fly the plane as if I'm not here".

Yes!

No.

He started giving me instructions again. Gutted. But then I realised his instruction was to stop half way up the runway on my next landing. THIS IS IT! I was excited more than you can possibly imagine as you read this, I had dreamt of this moment for years, I had gone over it in my head time and time again, I have enviously watched other people do it, and here it was, finally my turn. I stopped half way up the runway and Rich opened the door, got out of the plane and told me to fly one circuit on my own. He said I was very capable and would be fine and then asked me if I was ok? I have no idea what I said to him but I remember wearing my poker face that said - "Of course I am, get out of my plane and shut the door behind you".

He did. Oh no. Was I really ready? Is this stupid? It's been fun till now but as much as I felt confident in flying the plane, I always had the security blanket of Rich (or another instructor) sitting right next to me ready to step in if things went wrong. Now here it was, just me. Fear. I felt it. So I

told myself that Rich knew what he was doing, he believed in me and if he believed in me then I needed to believe in me. Full throttle. It was on. I lifted off and pushed the stick slightly forward to gain speed before climbing but suddenly I was taken by surprise, the plane shot straight up. Woah! I levelled it off and pulled the speed back a bit. Without being rude to Rich, the weight difference was massive in a small plane, it handled very differently. I was beyond five hundred feet now but I decided to make a larger circuit than before so I could make wider turns, it was bumpy and I was nervous, I don't remember if I was smiling or not. I looked down at the runway as I eventually flew downwind and my head went into overdrive. How did I get here? This is one of the most amazing and terrifying experiences of my life, it was a dream coming true that even I, as an optimist, possibly thought would never happen. Then it was time to turn on to base leg. Watching my GoPro film of this bit it shows that I did some sort of curved turn into final approach instead of flying a base leg, I don't remember that but clearly poker face was hiding the nerves inside. I landed (gently) and brought the plane to a halt next to Rich who was beaming.
"Well done mate, you did it!"
I was a bit overwhelmed to be honest. When we pulled up on the apron, the other pilots were there and also Santi the aerodrome owner and Effing Mike too. They were clapping and whooping. It was the best greeting ever, they had all done it too in the past and to this day remember every detail of their first solo flight. They then threw a bucket of water over me and cheered. Awesome. Great pictures. Santi shook my hand and said "Never forget, you flew your first

solo flight at my aerodrome".

I phoned my wife to tell her and the emotion of it all took over and a tear or two may have appeared, probably just because of the sweat running down my head. What a day, finally, I had done it. That evening they all raised a glass and then sang a rude song to me in French. What a day indeed.

Chapter 19

Fuel Up

The next day at breakfast Rich and I agreed the plan now was for me to get my ten solo hours in that I needed for my licence. We got in early, I prepped the plane, did the walk round and checked the fuel. It was below twenty litres, I needed a minimum of thirty litres, the plane uses around fifteen litres an hour and we always plan to have fifteen litres spare. Mr Grumpy was not available to refuel the plane so another guy called Bob, who was part of the new team setting up this new venture at Soria and also an instructor, offered to refuel. Rich came over to assist with manoeuvring the plane into position which I would be glad of shortly. With the side panel removed and Rich checking the level of the tank, I went round the other side to remove the fuel cap (a precious item never to be misplaced as some poor soul did when we were at Headcorn one time). Bob stuck the fuel nozzle in and squeezed the lever. Fuel shot all over the inside off the rear part of the plane, everywhere but in the fuel tank.
"STOP" Rich shouted.
We could smell it. Bob had pushed the fuel nozzle straight through the side of the pipe that leads to the tank. I think there would have been blood if Mr Grumpy had done this, thankfully Bob was a decent bloke who had just made a genuine mistake and meant no harm. Everyone gathered round to watch what was happening and I was a little perturbed when I noticed one of them was smoking a cigarette as they peered into the fuel soaked plane. I stepped back. Way back. Tools were found, the pipe was cut and

manoeuvred and careful refuelling now took place. I got in the plane. What a stink, I was nearly high before flying high. I was strangely calm now, all the calamity of the fuel spill had taken my mind off the fact I was about to go flying on my own in Northern Spain.

After my pre-flight checks, I started the plane on the apron. Richard's voice came over the radio.
"Radio check".
"It's a five, hearing you loud and clear".
"Golf Echo Delta, this is Richard, radio check please".
"Yes, five, all good, Echo Delta" I replied.
"Stuart, can you hear me?"
"Yes!"
I looked out the door, he was coming over. The aerodrome was using a small hand held radio for communication at the moment and Richard was holding it and looking agitated. This hadn't been a great morning for him so far, having his plane damaged and now his student can't communicate with him on the radio. I shut the engine down and he approached and opened the door.
"Can you not hear me?"
"Yes, I am replying"
"Well try pressing the com button when you reply!"
What a muppet. I have spent hours and hours with Richard's voice coming through my headphones and I just replied straight away because he is sitting next to me, but of course now he is in my headphones but not sitting next to me. Thankfully he let me proceed. I pulled on to the runway and for the first time got to announce:
"Student Golf Echo Delta entering runway two seven for immediate departure".

I had read my manuals, I knew that when you were flying solo without a licence you had to say "student" followed by the plane's registration. I was smiling again, this was another milestone reached. Bob, who had the fueling incident, told me some places to go and see and as soon as I took off I followed his instructions. I flew through what I can only describe as a very wide bowl, with a flat plain below and mountains either side. After about ten miles I came to some lakes in which there was an historic village below the water, apparently you can see the top of the church spire peering out of the water. I didn't see it but it was a beautiful area to fly over nonetheless. After an hour of flying I requested an extension which was granted and I flew some more. This was what it was all about, now I was really flying. I wasn't practising any manoeuvres or procedures, I was just flying, sightseeing over Northern Spain. Then suddenly my peace was broken.
"Echo Delta, Echo Delta, do you read?"
It was the unmistakable voice of Romain.
"Go ahead Romain, Echo Delta".
"What is your location?"
"Fifty miles South West of Soria, Echo Delta".
"You are out of radio range, you need to come back".
I turned the plane round and headed back. When I landed Rich was on the apron and he said to me over the radio "Do you want another hour?"
"I need the toilet first" I replied, and then I realised he was joking. When I got out of the plane Mike came up to me and asked "Where the ____ have you been?" He was genuinely perplexed.
"I was flying, it was all good and safe, I knew where I was

and where the aerodrome was" I replied, "Was Rich concerned?"
"I don't give a _____ if he was concerned, I was wondering where the _____ you'd got to, I was more worried about the plane to be honest and me getting my lessons".
We laughed.

Armed with coffees and an omelette we sat outside the cafe to eat and watched some aerobatic training flights. As we sat taking in the atmosphere, a lurid green old Cessna landed. It was a surprisingly shocking colour. Three large men got out, all looking rather hot and sweaty and ready for some refreshment. They had a short stop, a drink and some food and then all squeezed back in the plane. With what seemed like no pre-flight checks, the starter was pushed and the propellor started turning. And turning. The engine wasn't catching. By now the aerobatic plane was on the ground and we were all sitting outside having lunch so there was an audience watching the mean green machine. A very knowledgable audience too. Soon the advice started flowing. "Flooded the engine" "Has he switched the magnetos on?" The propellor was still turning. Eventually someone stood up, I think they were more concerned about the plane than the passengers, but they had had enough by now and decided to go and tell them to stop. Just as they got to the plane - boom, it roared in to life with a huge plume of smoke. Everyone cheered, but I think it was probably rather derisory. The plane then manoeuvred from the apron and on to runway two seven. You have to back track up runway two seven a fair way before turning round and lining up up for take off. The green machine stopped and turned round very early, surprisingly early. The mood changed at the cafe. Everyone stopped talking and all eyes were back on the Cessna.

"He's surely not going to try to take off from there?"
We all thought it, no one said it. Full power was applied and the plane started moving. We stood up. It went past us, surely not fast enough? By this point on the runway, all previous planes were fully airborne. The green machine was still rolling on the ground, it had three heavy people on board. Remembering all the scare stories I had been told earlier, I started to think this doesn't look good and looking at the expressions on the faces around me they were thinking the same thing. As it came to the end of the runway and was about to run on to the grass, it suddenly lifted, not high but just enough to get off the ground. We still watched. Slowly, very slowly, it gained height, the engine working flat out, eventually flying just over the road which was five hundred feet below everyone else by the time they had reached that same point. And breath. We all sat down and there was more than a few comments about how lucky (and stupid) they had been. Later that day Mike flew his first solo and was welcomed back and duly soaked by Romain. It was an honour to share that moment with Mike, and great we both did it on this trip.

I flew again in the afternoon and started clocking up the hours and was looking forward to flying again in the evening but it was not to be. At the start of the week there was an agreement made between the instructors that the gliders would stay to the North of the field. This worked for a bit but when the wind changed so did the gliders area of flying and they would fly wherever they wanted. Planes give way to gliders so we would have to change our areas of operation. All of the pilots in the planes made good use of the radio, constantly informing everyone of their movements. The gliders never made radio calls. This was causing some friction. The gliders were launched from a cable and occasionally the cable would land on the runway which caused a few issues, I aborted a landing at one point after being informed there was a cable on the runway as I was coming in to land. The final straw was when the gliding instructor started flying across the upwind section of the runway and then turned and flew down the runway to land in the direction we were all taking off from. He was basically flying in to the direction of any planes taking off or landing and he was still making no radio calls. He was doing this so the glider was at the starting point to launch again without having to walk it all the way down there. The instructors knocked heads. This was totally unacceptable apparently and would lead to an incident. There was a lot of steam let off and a lot of words exchanged. No more flying that day. Richard was not prepared to put his pupils in any more danger. I was bitterly disappointed but I have learned to trust that Rich has been in this game for years now and knows what he is talking about. You can't take chances in aviation. An unexpected end to another days flying.

Chapter 20

Home Time

The next day there were various meetings and discussions, decisions made and tempers now calmed down. I don't know what was agreed but I was flying again which was the main thing for me, I was running out of time now so wanted to fly as much as possible. Some more planes started arriving at the airfield, the first was the coolest looking plane which had come all the way from Germany, a pilot and his girlfriend who was bursting for the loo when they landed. Then another plane. And another. Apparently news was out in the wider aviation community about the goings on at Soria and a microlight club had all decided to come and visit. This meant I had to keep a good look out now when I was flying circuits and it's just as well I did. I had one more hour left to fly to get my ten hours in and Rich told me he wanted me to spend it doing circuits. So I headed out and all was going well until I did a touch and go, turned right into the crosswind leg and there was a stunning red biplane coming straight toward me, thankfully we knew our aviation law and both proceeded to turn right. He eventually joined me downwind and landed behind me. I carried on with another circuit. I was nearly there now, each circuit takes about ten minutes and I only need to do two more to reach my goal of ten hours solo flying for my licence. But more and more microlights were coming into the circuit and landing now and for some reason they were not making radio calls and to make things worse the gliding school had decided to start to use the radio now, not to inform us of their operations but to call to each other. In

French. Continually. It was not helpful.

"Echo Delta? Stuart? Do you copy?"

"Yes Romain, I hear you" I replied.

Romain was talking to me while he was looping upside down somewhere above us.

"Stuart, please make finals to land in this circuit, it is getting too dangerous now, too many planes coming in at once and no one is using the radio".

I was gutted, I knew this meant I would be ten minutes short. In the grand scheme of things this won't matter because I still had to do some more solo navigation when I got home but it was still my aim for this week and I now wasn't going to be able to fulfil it. I landed and pulled on to the apron to a stunning sight. These planes, classed as microlights, are absolutely stunning, especially the bi-plane. There was a ton of money here and it was shiny, there was even a flexwing which made me smile because this was my only image of a microlight flying originally. Even it looked stunning, £40,000 worth, the cheapest microlight there. Mike and I enjoyed looking at all the planes and then it was time for me to head to Malaga and get my flight home. I went into the cafe for a final coke and Mr Grumpy's wife was there serving. I ordered a sandwich and a drink and went to pay and she smiled and refused to take the payment. She then spoke to two trainee commercial pilots (who had also landed that same day with their instructor in three underwing microlights that they were learning in) and they translated to me that she apologised for her husband and his bad manners and said he really was a kind man at heart. She said she enjoyed us all being at the aerodrome and hoped we would come back soon. It was a good way to end. I said my goodbyes to everyone including my new friends. Romain gave me his white flying scarf, I had been pulling his leg about it during the week. It was a kind gesture from him and a good way to finish my trip. I told him I was going to put it on ebay to help pay for my lessons. He swore at me in French. And once again, we all laughed. I drove off in the midday heat in Mike's hire car and headed for Malaga. Foolishly, I followed Mike's advice not to go on the toll roads and headed into a three hour journey from hell. The road was empty. I went up hills, down hills, round twisty tight death trap corners on the edge of huge drops, the scenery would have been stunning if I hadn't just spent a week flying over beautiful countryside, and then horror of horrors, I was running out of fuel! There I was in the middle of nowhere, boiling hot sun and about to run out of fuel and miss my plane. And then die of thirst. This was not a good end. I saw a small group of buildings on a hill in the distance, similar to many I had been flying round, using as way points to stop me getting lost. What do I do now? Waste fuel driving into it or drive on. I drove into it. No fuel. I am driving on vapours now. I start praying. A Lot of praying. Then I pressed my phone to see if google maps was still running and it fell on to the floor. Great. I had to stop but when I picked it up a menu popped up and there I saw it had petrol stations listed. I pressed it, getting quite desperate now, and there it was, a petrol station, but it was eighteen minutes away. These were the longest eighteen minutes of my entire life. The needle stayed on empty the whole way. Eventually I opened the fuel cap in the petrol station and the car sucked in air expressing exactly how I was feeling.

Fuelled up, I headed off to the airport but when I got there it didn't go so smoothly either, maybe I was just tired, but I ended up driving round and round trying to find the hire car return. The bus drivers were getting a bit fed up with me as I slowed down at each exit trying to work out where I was going. It did seem a bit ironic that I had spent a whole week checking I had enough fuel to fly a plane and then navigating without a hitch for miles and miles in the sky yet here I am back in a car, nearly running out of fuel and I can't navigate to a car park. Finally after a few circuits (ground circuits now) of the airport, I found the hire place and returned the car. Eventually I boarded the plane, it seemed huge. It was. I sat at a window seat overlooking the wing and watched with renewed interest as the flaps were set for take off, this was a whole different type of flying, I had renewed respect for the pilots. I flew from Malaga back to Gatwick, completely shattered but very very happy from the most amazing adventure I had just been on. The flying, not the driving! As I walked out of customs I could see my family all together smiling waiting for me, it was a beautiful moment. The thoughts of writing goodbye letters before I left popped into my head and I smiled. Family hug in the airport.

"How was it?" Andy asked.

"Effing great!" I said. In my head. And laughed at my toast to Mike from Manchester.

Chapter 21

Cross Countries

I had flown for forty one hours and fifty six minutes in the C42 which included nine hours and fifty minutes of solo flying. All I needed to do now were two solo cross countries and the General Skills Test. I booked in with Rich to do my cross countries and he told me to prepare a PLOG (flight plan log) for a flight to Goodwood. This was good! I had wanted to fly to Goodwood for some time now and here it was about to happen. I got my map, ruler and protractor and made a plan, armed with the latest weather reports, I did some practise triangle of velocities to get my ground speeds and actual headings. All good, I remember! It had been a few weeks since the written navigation exam. Then I looked on google maps and followed the route from Deanland to Goodwood, taking in all the roads, Shoreham Airport, a quarry, Arundel Castle and even a passenger jet that google maps has captured in the picture. Hopefully I won't be seeing one of them at 2,200ft, my planned height, apparently lots of pilots fly at 2000ft so I choose to avoid this. The morning came, I got up early, read the Notam (notice to airmen) for the day to make sure nothing was happening on my chosen route. All good. I re did my PLOG with the current winds forecast for the day and then headed out to get my motorbike ready to head to Deanland. I was excited!! Then I got a text. I knew before looking at it that it was off. Weather was perfect so it must be something else. Shellie told me the plane had a flat tyre and Richard is stranded at Shoreham. Arg. I was keen to get it all wrapped up now and I want as little time as possible between flying so I don't have to relearn anything but I was going to have to be patient. We re arranged for a late lesson the following day. Late the following afternoon I headed to Deanland. We made a quick phone call to Goodwood because it is PPR (Prior Permission Required) and they informed us they close at 6pm sharp. It's 5pm and I hadn't prepped the plane. Thankfully Rich was well known to them and they gave permission as long as I could be in and gone by 6pm. "Prep the plane" he mouthed to me as he chatted on the phone to them.

I checked the plane over, all good, fuel? Plenty. Good. Rich gave me a sheet that needed to be filled in by the people at Goodwood to confirm my landing and procedures. I got in the plane, pre flight, lined up and I was off. Smiling. Lots! I hadn't flown since Spain. It is hard to describe this feeling, it is just amazing, freedom, the views, the machine, I absolutely love it. Driving over to the airfield I had had the doubts again - could I do this, was I crazy? Blah blah blah, all the voices. Noise! But the moment I was flying they were all gone. I could do this, this was meant to be. I headed to Goodwood aware of the time, but this was my first solo flight in the UK, it was a big deal for me. My house is not far off the route and I knew that if I got lost I could fly South a bit over the Downs and pick up the A27 which goes straight to Chichester via Goodwood. After flying over Glyndebourne Opera House, then Lewes, I followed the road to Hassocks. At Hassocks I saw my son's school and then followed the road in to Hurstpierpoint. I could see where new houses were being built and worked out where my road was from them. I spotted my neighbour's huge fir tree and lowered my height and started to circle. Kyle was on the trampoline. He spotted me first. As I flew round I could see Holly's friends out on the road stop and look up. I came round the back of the house again and Kyle was now joined by Holly and Andrea. They were waving. By now I'm sure you can guess how I was feeling. Huge smile! I tipped my wing and headed to Goodwood. It was all going well, the map matched with what was on the ground although the roads were smaller than I expected, due to lots of trees I guess. Just using a map made me feel quite exposed which I wasn't expecting. I flew all over Spain full of confidence but there I could see for miles and miles in every direction, the roads were clear, it was all very open. Now in the Sussex countryside it was hazy, you couldn't actually see a good horizon and the land was all green quilted. Strange. I avoided Shoreham airspace, because I wanted to keep this as simple as possible, and came to Arundel. Time to make my radio call. I did my best but it could have been better, they were actually very friendly sounding and put me at ease. I started with "Student" and they replied "Student" which meant I didn't have to keep saying it. The noise abatement procedure is very strict at Goodwood so I was expecting a forceful reminder but I didn't get one which actually helped my confidence and made me even more sure I would not mess up how I approached the circuit. On my current heading I was coming in on a long final to runway two eight, the runway in use and Goodwood information asked me how I intended to join, probably assuming I would join on a long final. The only problem was that I didn't actually know where the airfield and runway actually were yet, I was still following my map on my knee board so I informed them I would join overhead so I could see where I was going to land. They seemed ok with this. Then, as I was approaching where Goodwood should be, I could feel my stomach tensing up a little. Where is it? Will I find it? Thankfully looking at google maps really helped, I could see an area ahead with a small tower and some grass strips that I assumed must be the runways. I joined overhead at 2000ft, clearly saw the numbers two eight on the runway, and made my radio call. I followed the circuit joining downwind, base leg and called final. All exactly as I had pictured it over and over in my head. My landing was super smooth and I relaxed, got off the runway and parked up North of the tower as instructed. It was five minutes to six. I grabbed my sheet, ran up the tower, two people were there, very friendly. I handed the controller my sheet and he filled it in choosing - excellent - to the question - how was the students landing. Phew! He then opened his bottom drawer and pulled out a sticker sheet and stuck a gold star on it like you get in Kindergarten. Followed by a lot of laughing. He ran down the stairs with me and drove me to the office in a golf buggy to pay my landing fee. He then drove me back to plane and said he looked forward to me visiting Goodwood again when I had my licence. I said that I would as long as I got the same special treatment. Back in the plane I lined up at the end of the runway, made my radio call, got clearance and took off. He recommended I take the scenic route back along the coast and who was I to argue, it sounded like a good idea to me. Just then a call came in from another pilot asking for permission to land. He was cleared to land but reminded they closed at six. He made his call including that he had eyes on me heading to the coast. I banked round and watched him land a Spitfire. Awesome!

I was back at Deanland by 6.40pm, handed Rich my sheet and reminded him I only needed to do one more cross country on my own. He said the plane was being used by a hirer later that evening. I gave him the look of a poor little puppy. Effing Mike would have been proud of his reply.
"Oh for_____ sake, do a PLOG" he barked. He made the call to another airfield. No answer.
"Prep the plane!" He said, still waiting for an answer.
I grabbed the fuel and as I got to the plane, I finally heard someone answer. This was good! I could be done with one more big part of getting my licence by the end of tonight. I headed off again. Yes, I was smiling. Non stop. I followed the map very carefully. It's harder this time, I hadn't done this route on X PLane or looked at google maps to familiarise myself with what the ground route looks like from the air. Slightly nervous. About ten miles out from the airfield I made my radio call. No answer. This was not good. This field stays open till eight but I'm getting no reply. I double checked I was using the right frequency on my radio. All correct. I focused hard on getting to the field and hoped someone would answer soon, the only problem was that after following my heading for the correct amount of time I had ended up over a very large town and not the airfield. This was a very horrible feeling that I am guessing a lot of pilots have felt before me. I tried not to panic and instead followed my training - fly the plane. With the plane in trim I looked all around me and worked out from the map that I had drifted to the right. I turned left knowing that I hadn't come to a large river yet so I was not too far North. I made a radio call. No answer. My eyes were

outside the cockpit scanning the ground. Eventually I saw a field that looked well cut and long. Thankfully as I approached it I saw a number of light aircraft parked up, I was in the right place. There was no activity in the area or on the ground so after flying overhead at two thousand feet, I descended and joined downwind and made another radio call.

"Student Echo Delta, pass your message" came the reply through my headset. And relax. I got permission to land. In the control room the controller apologised to me and said they had had a funeral that day and he thought the field was closed for the evening. It was obviously a lot more somber than my experience at Goodwood. He signed and stamped my sheet. My take off this time was not the best. There was a sudden crosswind gust which caught me by surprise, thankfully it is a large runway and it wasn't a problem but it certainly was a good reminder to stay 100% focussed at all times. Now I had to find Deanland from a new direction, I also had a strong headwind which was a bit frustrating especially knowing that someone would be waiting to hire the plane as soon as I landed. Rich had drummed in to me to look after the plane by cruising at between 4,200rpm and 4,500rpm to stop the engine from overheating, so I just had to fly the plane at about 90 knots with a ground speed of probably only 70mph and hope the hirer wasn't too annoyed at being held up. Eventually I got back and had no trouble finding the field, I made my calls and landed. Landing is definitely one of the best bits of flying. It takes all of your concentration knowing you are going to land this machine on a small strip of grass ahead of you, and when it goes well it is very satisfying. Rich had informed me he wanted a nice low landing and not to mess it up especially if people were watching. No pressure. It went well. Cross countries done! I headed for home, mentally exhausted but feeling good.

Chapter 22

The Final Exam

All I needed to do now was to pass my General Skills Test and I would be a pilot. A journey that started so long ago was now very close to completion.
"This is really happening" I told my wife, "I am over the tipping point". I could start to tell myself it was no longer a dream, it was about to become a reality. If only it was that simple. I booked in with the examiner, Chris, the instructor I had my for my first lesson in the C42. After our pre-flight check in the morning which included checking the oil and the dip stick dripping a blob of oil on to my nice blue Soria Aerodrome shirt that I had worn specially today to at least make me look like a pilot, we spent a couple of hours doing some upper air work and a bit of revision. It all went well. He put the plane into unusual positions and I had no problem recovering it. I stalled the plane and recovered it. Then we stopped for some lunch, sandwiches and coffee, it seemed to be turning out to be a good day. After lunch we headed back off for a pre GST. The thing is, if the pre GST goes well it can be upgraded to a GST. It was on. I taxied the plane to the hold for runway two four, looked at the windsock which was showing about 200 degrees at 10 knots. I pulled the brakes on for my pre-flight checks and then Chris said "Are you going to park in to wind?".
I looked at him with a confused look on my face which then turned into a "what a muppet" look on my face as I realised that instead of turning into wind to do my pre-flight checks I had actually parked the plane facing the direction the windsock was blowing. I must have been

nervous. This was not a good start. It would not be a good finish either. As soon as we took off, Chris pulled the power and announced - engine failure! I pushed the nose forward to stop the plane stalling and looked for a place to land. I gently turned to the right and informed him I was going to land in a particular field. Full power. We're off.
"Gold star!" He said.
Another one? I must be good at this I thought to myself. Too soon. We went through various other tests and it all seemed to go well. Then At around 1800 ft Chris pulled the power again and announced "Engine failure". I dipped the nose and re trimmed to keep the plane flying.
"Where is the wind coming from?" He asked.
"South west" I reply.
"Where are you going to land then?"
I pointed to a field nearby and start heading for it.
"Which field?"
I could tell he was agitated, I pointed to the field again.
"We are still at 1500 ft, how are you going to get us down there?"
I told him I was going to do a figure of eight at one end to lose height. He was clearly not impressed with this at all and put the power back on.
"Let's try this again shall we".
This was not good. I could feel a bead of sweat running down the side of my head.
"Engine failure!"
I re trimmed and looked for a field.
"Where are you going to land?"
I pointed to a field.
"Uphill??????!!!!!!"

It didn't look uphill to me.

"Let's go back to the airfield" he said.

We headed back in silence. I was absolutely gutted. Defeat. I hated it. Thankfully despite the pressure I made a very gentle landing, maybe that will cheer him up.

"Well, that was a pre GST" he told me as we got out of the plane. I felt sick.

My wife text me and asked how it was going and told me that we had been invited to a BBQ that evening. I text back - "I failed". I couldn't say anything else. I was drained, physically and emotionally. Rich had told me about when people pass their test there are often tears, some people just collapse after all the pressure and cry. I had wondered how I would react after this journey. At that moment I could have just walked away from it all. Strange reaction but it was how I felt in the moment. Someone from the office phoned Chris and must have asked how it was going. He informed them what we had done and then replied to another question, "I don't know, there is still time if Stuart wants to go up again". I really couldn't face going through all that again but as soon as he said it I knew that I was going to do it. There was no point in arguing with myself, I knew I was going to say yes. I started to prep the plane and discovered we had used up all the fuel. Nuts. We had to jump in to Chris's car and head to the petrol station. This gave us both a chance to unwind. He asked me about my figure of eight for the forced landing and I explained to him that I had read about it the night before. In my head I was going to do exactly what the textbook had shown me. Chris explained to me this was not a good first option and I needed a better plan. He was of course right and this was a valuable part of my learning. We eventually headed off again. Back through all the procedures I had done before. He even had me doing short field take offs which was actually fun and a light escape from the tension. Brakes on full, then full power, release the brakes and whoosh, you are off. Literally. Loved it. Then came the bit we both knew was coming. "Engine failure!" I was too spent to panic or be nervous now. Also, I had a good picture in my head of what was expected of me this time round. I chose a field much further away and started a circuit to that field eventually turning into the wind for a final approach at around 600ft. I would easily make it. We glided down and I prepared to land. "Full power". Off we went. Success. Relief. When we landed Chris shot a load of questions at me. I struggled a little due to tiredness but did ok overall. He reached out his hand. I paused. Was this really it? How was I going to react? I shook it and he said, "Well done". Strangely, I had no reaction other than a polite thank you. I really was exhausted by now. I should have sat down and had a cup of tea but I don't drink tea, instead I jumped on my bike and headed to the BBQ. My family wasn't there yet. My friends asked how my day had been and I don't remember what I said, I was in a bit of a daze and definitely dehydrated. Eventually Holly and Kyle appeared and gave me a big hug. I had forgotten that the last message they got was "I failed" so they were probably not sure what to expect. Andrea appeared at the gate, (looking even more gorgeous now), she stopped and gave me a look of apprehension. I put my arms round her and with some emotion and relief I said "I passed".

Chapter 23

Where's My Licence?

It had taken me just under two months to get my National Private Pilot's Licence, the fastest so far at the flying club. I then had an agonising three week wait for the Civil Aviation Authority to send it through to me, I can't actually hire a plane until I physically have the licence in my hand. During this time I had the opportunity to fly a passenger jet in a proper simulator. This was quite an experience. Landing was very different from what I had been taught. On the C42 as soon as you know you are going to make the runway you pull the power and glide down. I did this on the passenger jet and fell out of the sky and landed tail first and hard on the runway, so much so that my gopro flew off of it's mount and landed on the floor. Also, on the C42, when you land on the back wheels, you hold the nose up as long as possible which acts as an air break and helps to slow you down, whereas on the passenger jet you actually have to push the yoke forward to force the nose down. I sat there in the captain's seat in the simulator and in my heart I knew that I would love to be doing this full time. I once said to a friend that being an airline pilot must be the best job in the world and he totally disagreed with me saying it was just a glorified bus driver. But what an awesome bus I thought to myself. Leaving the simulator, I told myself not to think about what might have been but instead focus on what is happening now. I remembered something my son Kyle told me a couple of months ago just before I started learning on the C42. We were at a Christian conference called Spring Harvest at Butlins in Minehead, I was working and my family were with me and enjoying a holiday. Kyle had been to a seminar where the speaker asked the kids if they had a dream about their future, something they really wanted to do. Most of them put their hands up to say yes. He then asked them "What are you going to do today to make that dream come closer to reality?". I was very challenged by this and it has stuck with me to this day, and in my moment where I could have looked back at what I hadn't done, I chose instead to focus on what I actually had done, the fact that I had just managed to finally get my NPPL. No it's not a commercial pilot's licence but it is still a licence to fly. Whenever people have talked to me about flying during these past couple of months they have all, without exception, asked the same question - "So what's the plan?" I have found this a hard question to answer because to me the plan was obvious - get a pilot's licence. That in itself would be an amazing achievement for me. Then they would say "Yes, but you have to keep flying or you will lose it." I had an answer for that question. After two years of holding a licence, you need to get it revalidated. To do this, you must have flown 12 hours in the previous 12 months including 12 take offs and landings. I had asked about hire cost at the start of my course and it was £80 an hour so this seemed achievable. Some people asked me if it was a career change. I would love to make a living from flying, but to get a commercial pilot's licence would take a lot of money and time and there is a a lot of competition for any job within the aviation industry. So what's my plan? Well it was to get a licence, then, to keep the licence which seemed like a good plan to me. As the days went by and the post came and went without any licence turning up, I was keen to fly.

So I arranged to do a supervised solo flight. This means you have to pay for an instructor who stays on the ground but is in radio contact with you the whole time. Hoping my licence would turn up beforehand, I tried to book for a week Monday or Tuesday neither of which were free. So it was booked for Friday. There was still a chance my licence would arrive. Friday came but the licence didn't. I headed off for my supervised solo. Rich met met me at the clubhouse and asked where I was planning on going. I pointed over my shoulder. "Gatwick?" he asked, "Why not" I replied, "What could possibly go wrong?" We both laughed.

My daughter, Holly, was camping with friends near Bolney so I flew from Deanland, over Lewes, Hassocks, Hurstpierpoint and found the A23, turned right and followed it to Bolney. After a few turns I found her campsite. Holly and her friends came out of the food tent and jumped up and down waving to me. I flew round them then tipped my wing as I flew off. That was a good moment. I then flew from Bolney down the A23 to Brighton. I watched a huge tailback for about three miles caused by a car fire just before the roundabout at the end of the A23 as you come in to Brighton. I flew over Brighton looking down at all the houses and parks, it really is a great city (all be it a small "city"). When I reached the seafront I turned left and flew along the beach looking down at everyone enjoying their day by the sea, it felt good, I had sat on Brighton beach many times and watched light aircraft flying along the coastline, I'm sure the pilots were smiling and content just as I was feeling at that moment. I flew over Brighton Pier and then on to the Marina, it was a beautiful day. Eventually I passed by Newhaven and turned left before Seaford, flying through a small wisp of misty cloud from the sea, and headed back towards the airfield. I made my radio calls and joined the circuit downwind for runway two four, turned right on to the base leg at Ringmer, then right again over the camper van shop on to a dog leg final back in to Deanland. I knew Rich would be watching closely and I also knew there were a number of people at the new clubhouse which is right at the end of the runway but I was too happy to feel any pressure. The wind was gusting 15 knots straight down the runway so it wouldn't be a problem. I brought the plane in nice and low and gently touched down holding the nose in the air to scrub off some speed and then the front wheel came gently down. It couldn't have gone better, landing is definitely one of the most enjoyable parts of flying, at least when it goes well. By the time I got to the end of the runway I had released the flaps and switched off the fuel pump. I brought the plane round to the parking spot, checked the magnetos at 2000rpm, switched off the transponder and radio, throttle to minimum and then switched off the two magnetos one after the other, the shut down procedure now committed to memory. Rich greeted me with his usual wide grin, "How was it mate?" "Brilliant as always" I replied. We headed in to the new clubhouse and Rich proceeded to show me his new plans - a flight simulator. He was buying it from Ireland, I think he said it was going to cost about £60,000 and he was going to put it in the old office. We watched some videos of it on youTube, it looked amazing. I told him I had a friend who used to work for the CAA and his job was to licence simulators. Rich was excited by this news and asked me to bring him over "for a coffee". I said absolutely, as long as he gave me Bruce Dickinson's phone number. Bruce (lead singer of Iron Maiden) is flying mad and owns a 747 and a huge simulator and also happens to be a good friend of Rich's.

"No probs" says Rich, "Have you got your phone?" I pulled out my phone, Rich looks up the Bruce's number on his phone, "Ready?" asks Rich, "Ready" I confirmed.......... "Dream on mate" he laughed.

Then he said "Come and check this out". We headed over to the other side of the airfield and there was a class A single engine plane, wings underneath, similar to a PA28, glass cockpit, it looked lovely. "I am thinking of buying this to hire out, what do you think?"

"It looks stunning, and fast" I replied.

"It is" said Rich, "You could do a three hour session and get this added to your license".

I told Rich my plans were to spend a year flying the C42 and get some good experience before doing anything else. We headed back to the clubhouse. I was amazed yet again at Rich's enthusiasm for all things flying and his schemes and plans, there was never a dull moment with him. Unfortunately, this would turn out to be the last time I would ever see Rich. The following morning my licence arrived, and with hindsight I am glad it was delayed a day or I may have just hired out one of the planes from Shellie and never got that last chance to hang out with Rich.

Chapter 24

I Have A Licence

It was finally time. I had my licence, I could now hire the plane and fly. No instructor, no nerves, I had the document in my hand that confirmed I could fly. Just like the Tin Man, The Lion and the Scarecrow in the Wizard of Oz, when Dorothy gives them certificates to say they have brains or no fear etc I now have a licence that says "You can do this!". I don't have to listen to any voice of fear saying "You're not good enough". So I contacted the club to book my first hire for this Sunday coming, finally it won't cost me as much now that I'm not paying for an instructor. And then I'm knocked back again. Turns out there is a substantial annual membership fee to paid up front, that alone will stop me flying soon, my Flying account is well and truly empty now. There is also a monthly subscription, fuel costs added, a landing fee added and then 20% VAT on top of everything now because the school had become so successful. I won't be flying on Sunday. Instead I am reminded of a T-shirt I saw in the Flightstore catalogue that said - "Welcome to the world of aviation, you are now broke". I am gutted as I read the email, my fault, I obviously misunderstood and wasn't aware of all the extras. I have spent my budget on getting my licence, I even sold my treasured PRS Single Cut electric guitar, possibly one my of my all time favourites, to help fund my lessons. As I read the email, I looked round my studio wondering if I had anything left I could sell. Unfortunately not. At this point I nearly named this chapter - It's Off Again - referring to earlier chapters in the book, but the thing I have learned from this whole experience is that if you want something bad enough then there is no magic wand, you just have to work even harder to make it happen. A few months ago I read about a young man who was so desperate to learn to fly that he took on an extra job delivering milk in the early hours of the morning to pay for his lessons. That challenged me to ask myself "Do I really want to do this or not". Two days ago I was at my son Kyle's award day at school and as I watched him walk up on stage to receive his award I read words written on the school hall wall - "Do not judge me by by my successes, judge me by how many times I fell down and got back up again" Nelson Mandela. I also read an article on a website that quoted Geoff Hill, the editor of Microlight Flying Magazine. In the article he said he has a part share in a small plane and pays £50 a month to cover hangarage, maintenance and insurance and then about £22 for every hour he flies it, so affordable flying is possible after all if you are prepared to search it out and find like minded people. The hunt is on. This truly has been an up and down adventure, both physically and emotionally. I have no idea what the future holds but I do know that right at this moment on the desk beside me is my NPPL Licence, I finally did it and yes, I am still smiling.

Richard Foster

I write this on August 4th 2017 sitting in a caravan back at Le Pas Opton in France where I had first announced to my wife that I wanted to get my pilot's licence and also the day after finishing writing this book. It is with great sadness I learned that my flying instructor and good friend Richard Foster passed away this morning. He had a great heart for life and for people but unfortunately it was his heart that let him down at the age of thirty nine, truly shocking for all who knew him and especially his family. Richard was an inspiration to many many people and someone who made people's dreams come true including mine, there are not many people you can say that about. In the short time I knew Rich he had a huge impact on me. One of my best memories is of him singing Kum By Ah to me as we flew over France, he thought this was highly amusing. Richard didn't just teach flying, he enthused it, he wanted his students to not only just succeed but to succeed well and be the very best pilots they could be. He was also a very generous person, he gave my daughter Holly a Flight Sport Aviation jacket for free because it was too small for the shop but it fitted her perfectly. He was also generous with his time and would stop and talk to anyone for as long as they wanted to talk, he never seemed impatient with people. After spending so many hours with Rich doing intense training and then letting our hair down (well, he could do that, mine blew away years ago) in the evening, it is hard to imagine flying without Richard being part of it. He was not only passionate about the flying, he loved the whole aviation community and everything that goes with it. I will miss him very much, we had become good friends.

Printed in Great Britain
by Amazon